Patricia Isabella Arrieta

UNDERSTANDING
yourself
Patricia Beall Gruits

God knows your purpose.
Do you?

PeterPat Publishers, Inc.

P.O. Box 081816
Rochester, MI 48308-1816

All scripture quotations are taken from
King James Version
unless otherwise noted.

UNDERSTANDING YOURSELF

Copyright © 2002 by Patricia Beall Gruits
First Edition, 2002

Library of Congress
ISBN 0-9639461-4-5

For information, address:
PeterPat Publishers, Inc.
P.O. Box 081816
Rochester, MI 48308-1816

Printed in the U.S.A.

"*For I know the plans
I have for you,
declares the Lord...
Plans to give you hope
and a future.*"

Jeremiah 29:11

Dedication

Dedicated to my eight grandchildren:

Matthew, Christopher, Allison,
Jennifer, Harry, Andrew,
Patricia and Jay Peter

*May this book help you to find
God's plan for your life.*

ACKNOWLEDGMENTS

*A*s far back as I can remember, I have regularly attended church services and heard famous men and women preach the Gospel. The Holy Spirit implanted *the Word* I heard in my spirit; He stored *truth* in my memory. I praise the Lord for this priceless treasure. How I wish I could remember and acknowledge all the saints whom the Lord used to enrich *my life with treasures old and new.*

When I shared my notes and thoughts gathered over several years on this subject, Kenneth and Bette Staugaard and Burnell and Mary Odoerfer encouraged me to write and teach "Understanding Yourself" to the Minister Candidate School.

After writing and successfully teaching these lessons for three years, Alvin and Linda Lawrence, Joy Gruits, Judy Bogrette, Bill and Tracy Cuppy and Susan Bulat volunteered to edit the material. William and Nancy Gruits prepared the final copy for publication. A very special 'Thank you and God bless you' to everyone who had a part in making this book possible.

Patricia Beall Gruits

INTRODUCTION

*U*nderstanding Yourself was written to help you discover and understand the plan and purpose of God for you. Your life is significant. You are more than a grain of sand on the seashore of life. Your life will have *meaning* and *purpose* when you find the *reason* for your existence.

I began writing *Understanding Yourself* when I lived in South Florida. I had begun a study on Life Missions and found it very stimulating and challenging. I eagerly shared what I had found with a group of Christian friends, who were earnestly seeking to know and fulfill the *purpose* of God for their lives. The more we shared, the more I researched for further insight into God's plan for His people.

Over the following years I spent many, many days in prayer and study researching for material to write in a book. I believe the material in *Understanding Yourself* will help people who are looking for *fulfillment* and an *answer* to the problems of life.

How can I know the will of God for my life? is not a new question. I had personally dealt with this question for many years. I remember when I was a student in bible college, that it was the biggest question among the student body; they were looking for an answer as to why they were there. Some students expressed fear. They were afraid of what the

Lord might ask them to do or where He would ask them to go. They reasoned, what we don't know, we can't be held responsible to do.

THERE IS AN ANSWER

During World War II, the families and friends of men in the military service *faithfully* prayed and attended church services, but when the war was over church attendance waned. The moving of the Holy Spirit had all but disappeared from many congregations. Churches across America were experiencing a spiritual drought.

Many old-timers expressed alarm as they recalled the good old days. They encouraged the ministers and converts to pray for a fresh visitation of God. In our local church, daily prayer was made to God for seven years for an outpouring of the rain from heaven to fall on the thirsty ground of men's hearts.

The Lord heard the cry of spiritually hungry people and a rain from heaven began to fall in 1947-48 and quickly spread throughout much of the world. When revival came to our home church the spiritual gift of prophecy with the laying on of hands began to operate and the Lord revealed, through His prophets, the life mission He had for His church. People came from everywhere to hear what God had *predestined* for their life. It was exciting! However, we soon learned these revival truths were not a cure-all. Just *hearing* about God's will and plan is not enough. The Word of the Lord must fall on good soil before it will take root and produce a bountiful crop. It always takes a concerted effort of *obedience* and *preparation* to fulfill the will of God for our life.

Ever since the Fall of Man, mankind has had a need, a craving to know the *purpose* and *plan* for his existence. It wasn't always that way. When God created man and woman the line of *communication* between them and their Creator was open, and they enjoyed *fellowship* together at the end of every day.

Life in Eden was perfect, complete; they knew their life *mission* and enjoyed it. But life in Eden had the *challenge* of obedience. The Creator warned them of one *restriction*: "Do not eat the fruit of the tree in the midst of the Garden, *the tree of Knowledge of Good and Evil.* The day you eat of that fruit, you will most surely die!"

When God created Adam and Eve, and all mankind He gave them a *free will*; they had the right to choose. The challenge of obedience was not to eat the forbidden fruit and it became a *nagging* temptation, hard to resist. We don't know *when* it happened but one day they were put to a *test*. *Lucifer*, the tempter, entered into a pet serpent to entice them, "Eve, this fruit will make you *super* wise. You won't need God for anything anymore. You will have all the answers. This fruit will make you so *independent*, you won't need God".

> *Let no one say when he is tempted, "I am tempted by God": for God cannot be tempted by evil, nor does He Himself tempt anyone. But each one is tempted when he is drawn away by his own desires and enticed. Then when desire has conceived, it gives birth to sin: and sin, when it is full-grown, brings forth death. (James 1:13-15)*

The desire to be *independent*, to be their own person, apart from God, was something they *desired* and *lusted for*; their act of disobedience was *deliberate*. Eating the forbidden fruit was a premeditated, conscious act, to sever their dependence on God. What they did not realize was that eating the forbidden fruit canceled their *covenant with God* and *sealed* a covenant with Lucifer.

The knowledge they received from Lucifer was experimental - sensual and devilish. Suddenly, they discovered their covering of innocence was gone; they were *naked*. So man was cast out of the very place where eternal life was within his grasp. But though barred from it, he has never ceased to remember it, to yearn for it, and to try to reach it.

SPIRITUAL AMNESIA

Since the Fall all mankind has suffered with "spiritual amnesia." We have lost our connection with our Creator. We have lost the knowledge of *who* we are, *what* we are or *why* we are. This was why Jesus Christ was sent to earth... to *reconcile* and *reconnect* us back to God.

Mankind is still struggling to be *independent of God*, and it leads him nowhere. "It isn't in man to choose his own way!"

Christ has been knocking at the door of your heart for a long time. Sometimes we recognize His knock and invite Him to come in and communicate to us His *love*, His *plan* and His *purpose* for our lives. But most of the time we ignore His knock and fail or refuse to open the door to Him. But He keeps on knocking and knocking and knocking.

Behold, I stand at the door and knock. If any man will hear my voice and open the door, I will come in to him, and sup with him, and he with me. (Rev. 3:20)

It is my prayer that you will recognize His knock and open the door of your heart and invite Him in. A wonderful life awaits us when we walk in agreement with God.

I have attempted to help my readers to *Understand Yourself*, to reconcile and be reconnected to God. It is my prayer that each chapter will help you understand God's great plan of salvation and restoration, to help you find your *mission* for life.

Patricia Beall Gruits

"Before I formed you
in the womb I knew you;
Before you were born
I sanctified you..."

Jeremiah 1:5

Table of Contents

Chapter		Question Numbers	Page
1	A Search to Understand Yourself	1-14	1
2	Be Reconciled to God	15-26	15
3	The Miracle of Pentecost	27-41	27
4	A New Heart and A New Spirit	42-53	41
5	The Testing of Our Faith	54-63	55
6	Freedom through Forgiveness	64-80	69
7	Failure Isn't Fatal	81-92	83
8	Your Family Tree	93-109	95
9	Make Me A Servant	110-121	109
10	Faith and Patience	122-132	123
11	Discovering Your Gifts	133-145	135
12	The River of God	146-160	149
13	Surviving Adversity	161-172	163
14	The Sanctified Self Image	173-184	173
15	Beyond Ourselves	185-196	187
16	Crossing The Finish Line	197-213	199

CHAPTER ONE

A Search To Understand Yourself

O Lord, you have searched me and known me.
You are acquainted with all my ways. (Ps. 139:1,3)

*T*here is a widespread interest for self-understanding and a hunger for self-esteem. It is not a secular fad that will go away. It rises from a human need, a hunger for identity. Man has a hunger to believe in himself, a need that drives him to *search* for a reason for his existence on earth. Something is missing in his life, and he doesn't know quite what it is, where he missed it, or how he can find it.

It all goes back to Adam and Eve's tragic fall from glory to disgrace. The first sinless human was made in the image of God and was "crowned with glory and honor". Man was God's masterpiece. God created him to play a lead role in the drama of history. Adam belonged to the royal family of God; it was his birthright.

All was well until Adam and his wife wanted to be *independent* of God, free from His *guidance* and *Lordship* over them. The serpent's offer of freedom, discovery and fulfillment, *independent* of God, was *irresistible*. They responded to the temptation to be free from God's control and partook of the forbidden fruit.

Suddenly, a new sense of inadequacy overtook them. They were stricken with the awful truth that all they could count on was wrapped up in themselves. Having rejected their spiritual dimension, they were now *totally dependent* on each other. They were aware for the first time that having declared themselves independent of God *left them only with the physical*. Their bodies were now all they had, and they *were naked*.

When Adam and Eve left the Garden of Eden, they walked out with guilt, shame and fear; they had lost both their royal identity and their dignity. The Adam who walked out of the garden was not a humble man. He was a humiliated human. He had lost his glory and self-esteem.

Ever since the "Fall of Man" every human being ever born has been torn apart with this *hunger* for lost glory, driven to recover his self respect.

1.   WHAT HAS MAN SUBSTITUTED FOR HIS LOST GLORY?

Man has a hunger to believe in himself, a need that drives him to search for a reason for his existence on earth. Man had to invent something to take the place of his God-given pride, so he manufactured a substitute we call **"ego"**.

Webster defines **ego** as "The 'I' or self of any person in self-importance, self-image, or self-esteem - having or regarding the self as the center of all things." Man's ego is a defense mechanism to find a way to hide his guilt and shame.

2. IS IT IMPORTANT FOR MAN TO FIND HIS SELF-IDENTITY?

Yes. Man is motivated to search for self-understanding by his innate desire for some reassurance of his uniqueness. We need to know our life has importance, that we are more than a statistic, more than just a number in the game of life. We need to know that God created us and put us here for a *reason*.

Human beings have always been and will always be incurably religious, because God has placed spirituality deep within our souls. We cannot fight it, ignore it, or run away from it. Intuitively, we look for a *faith* or *philosophy* that will relieve us of the pain of *separation* from our Creator.

3. HOW DOES A POOR SELF-IMAGE AFFECT US?

Personal worth is not something human beings are

free to take or leave. We must have it, and when it is unattainable, we suffer. We live in the age of "the walking wounded." Millions carry the scars of severe mental, emotional, sexual or physical abuse. Whether real or imagined, the majority of people are struggling to some degree with their self-image. No one can argue that the problem is very real and very overwhelming.

4.   CAN PSYCHIATRY AND PSYCHOLOGY HELP US?

At best, they can help you cope. Psychologists and psychiatrists may be able to evaluate your problem and help you understand why you are the way you are. They are relatively incapable of helping you deal with the root causes of all your problems or bringing you to ultimate healing.

5.   IS THERE A REMEDY?

Yes. Jesus Christ, the Son of God, was sent to earth to restore and to reconcile man to God. He gave His life as an atonement (payment) for our sins. Christ's death on the cross made *peace* with God so man could be reconciled and be assured of eternal adoption into His royal family.

6. HOW DOES OUR ADOPTION BY GOD AFFECT US?

When we are adopted into the family of God, we become the children of God, joint-heirs with Jesus Christ, with a royal identity and an *eternal* birthright.

This healthy spiritual sense of well-being is what every person in the whole world needs and seeks in his pursuit of self-esteem. Our friendship with God in Jesus Christ gives us *value*. It is based on our relationship as human beings who are *restored* to God through Jesus Christ.

> *But when the fullness of time was come, God sent forth His Son, made of a woman, made under the law, to redeem them that were under the law, that we might receive the adoption of sons. And because ye are sons, God hath sent forth the Spirit of His Son into your hearts, crying, Abba Father. Wherefore thou art no more a servant, but a son; and if a son, then an heir of God through Christ. (Gal. 4:4-7)*

7. WHAT IS THE GOSPEL'S MESSAGE?

The saving message of the Gospel is - **I belong to Jesus Christ!** We can say without hesitancy, "I am loved by God. I am a member of His royal family. I am somebody wonderful."

Our new identity gives us *confidence* that now we can do something and be somebody of profound value and worth to Jesus Christ in this world. Our pride is rooted in a redemptive relationship with Christ, and our *bond of kinship* is total, healthy and assured. We can't take credit for it. We owe it all to Christ and His cross.

> *I can do all things through Christ who strengthens me. (Phil. 4:13)*

> *But as many as received him, to them gave he power to become the sons of God, even to them that believe on his name: Which were born, not of blood, nor of the will of the flesh, nor of the will of man, but of God. (John 1:12, 13)*

8. DID GOD CREATE US FOR SOME UNIQUE REASON?

Yes! We were all created for God's pleasure, to give Him fellowship and to bring Him glory. In order for mankind to do this, God planned and assigned to every man and woman a *unique mission* for them to accomplish during their sojourn on earth.

> *For we are his workmanship, created in Christ Jesus unto good works, which God hath before ordained that we should walk in them. (Eph. 2: 10)*

> *Thou art worthy, O Lord, to receive glory and honor and power: for thou hast created all things,*

and for thy pleasure they are and were created. (Rev. 4:11)

9. WHAT IS MEANT BY YOUR LIFE MISSION?

Webster defines **mission** as "the special task for which a person is apparently destined in life, a continuing task or responsibility that one is destined or fitted to do or specially called upon to undertake."

Your life mission is the task God planned and assigned to you to accomplish on earth. You have a calling which exists *only* for you and which *only* you can fulfill. It *represents* the very essence of who you are. It *expresses* what you are all about. It is an overall theme which *guides* your life.

God graciously endowed you with certain aptitudes and abilities to accomplish your mission successfully. It takes *faith* in your Creator to recognize that inner voice and *courage* to respond. Being faithful to your mission is the only way to lead a rewarding life.

10. WHEN AND WHERE DID YOUR MISSION ORIGINATE?

God, who *knew* us before our birth, assigned us our special mission. We do not know when or where God decided our mission in life, but the Bible teaches God chooses, ordains and predestines men and women for *special tasks* on earth before they are born.

7

Because our mission in life on earth was planned by and originated with God, it is not unreasonable for us to suppose God created our soul, with its mission, before it entered our body. The Bible teaches us our birth is not our *real beginning* nor will our *death be the end.* Indeed, we all came from God and shall return to Him at death to give Him an accounting of the deeds we accomplished on earth.

The Lord said to me, I knew you before you were formed within your mother's womb; before you were born I sanctified you and appointed you as my spokesman to the world. (Jer. 1:4 LB)

According as He hath chosen us in Him before the foundation of the world, *that we should be holy and without blame before him in love: having predestinated us unto the adoption of children by Jesus Christ to Himself, according to the good pleasure of his will. (Eph. 1: 4,5)*

11. HOW DID GOD EXPECT MAN TO ACCOMPLISH THIS?

Men and women were originally created to *desire* communion with God. The purpose for this was to give them comfortable access to Him for the wisdom they needed to *understand* their mission. God would provide the instructive guidance to accomplish it. David wrote in the Psalms that God gave us talents and special skills to accomplish our mission; they

8

were woven into our members and written in His book.

I will praise thee; for I am fearfully and wonder-fully made: marvelous are thy works; and that my soul knoweth right well. My substance was not hid from thee, when I was made in secret, and curious-ly wrought in the lowest parts of the earth. Thine eyes did see my substance, yet being unperfect: and in thy book all my members were written, which in continuance were fashioned, when as yet there was none of them. (Ps.139: 14-16)

O Lord, I know that the way of man is not in him-self: it is not in man that walketh to direct his steps. (Jer. 10:23)

Man's goings are of the Lord; how can a man then understand his own way? (Prov. 20:24)

12.   WHY DON'T WE ALL KNOW OUR MISSION?

When Adam and Eve declared their *independence* from God, they sinned. Sin separated them from their Creator, and they lost their knowledge of God and His life mission for them. Consequently, all their *rebel-lious* descendants are separated from God and wander on planet Earth with "spiritual amnesia", not having any memory of their origin or knowledge of their destiny.

However, man needs a relationship with God in order

to be the unique human being he was created to be. It has been said, *"Religion or faith is the hard reclaiming of knowledge we once knew as a certainty."* *(Unknown)*

> *For all have sinned, and come short of the **glory** of God.* *(Rom.3:23)*

13. WHAT WILL THE DISCOVERING OF MY LIFE MISSION DO FOR ME?

Discovering your mission will give you purpose and direction for life, for it will put you in touch with that special God-given assignment only *you* are qualified to fill. Your heart will be flooded with light, so that you can see something of the future He has called you to share.

> *Moreover, because of what Christ has done we have become gifts to God that he delights in, for as part of God's sovereign plan we were chosen from the beginning to be his, and all things happen just as he decided long ago. I pray that your hearts will be flooded with light, so that you can see something of the future he has called you to share.* *(Eph.1:11,18 LB)*

> *Ye are a chosen generation, a royal priesthood, an holy nation, a peculiar people; that ye should shew forth the praises of him who has called you out of darkness into (his) marvelous light.* *(I Peter 2:9)*

10

14. CAN WE IDENTIFY OUR MISSION AND FIND OUR LOST GLORY?

Yes. Some fortunate people are *aware* of their life mission at an early age, others begin to recognize it in mid-life, and some find it in their golden years. Finding your mission will illuminate your way like a beacon. It will truly be "a light unto your pathway".

The important thing is to seek and then *carry out* your assignment. You can have an amazing self-image transplant, you can be *born again*. A mission achieved is *never* too late.

Adam's one sin brought the penalty of death to many, while Christ freely takes away many sins and gives glorious life instead. Yes, Adam's sin brought punishment to all, but Christ's righteousness makes men right with God, so that they can live.
(Rom. 5: 16,18 LB)

*God alone knows
how to instruct man
to fulfill his mission
successfully.*

CHAPTER TWO

Be Reconciled To God

...We implore you on Christ's behalf;
be reconciled to God. (2 Corinthians 5:20)

W hen Adam and Eve rebelled against God's guidance and care in their life, they cut themselves off from the flow of divine life that endowed them with glory, wisdom and power. In their blind desire for independence, they *ignored* the fact that a constant flow of this divine life by the Spirit is as *necessary* to man's spiritual life as light and water are to the continued life of a plant. Their rebellious move for independence alienated them from God's presence. Instant spiritual death was the result.

When Adam and Eve made their move to declare their independence from God, they unknowingly sided with Satan to become his slaves to evil and sin. *Whomever you yield yourself a servant to obey, his servant you become.* In man's continual struggle for self-dependence, he has made God his enemy.

Man has defiantly cooperated with the forces of evil to edge God out of the universe and human affairs. This estrangement from God has brought grievous trouble and sorrow to the entire human race, and to God.

It has been *apparent* from the beginning, man **does not** get along just as well without God. Though civilization has made remarkable advances in certain areas, we remain a most restless, uncertain and ungodly generation. Man's inability to control his own inner self has increased world tension. It is plain enough that in morals or in the basic ingredients of life, such as peace, happiness, and good will among men, man has failed miserably.

We are alarmingly plagued with high divorce and illegitimacy rates, a restless youth in frequent riots, and a persistence of the same old frustration . . . the *emptiness* of life without a divine *purpose.* Try as he may, man may never "come of age," in the sense that he no longer needs God. Man cannot make it on his own. The only answer to uncontrollable problems is to get back to a proper relationship with the unchangeable and ever-loving Creator.

15. WHAT HAS BEEN DONE TO RECONCILE GOD AND MAN?

God loved man so much that He sent His Son, Jesus Christ, to earth to die on the cross for man's sins; He bought man's pardon. Christ died for the sins of the world so mankind could be forgiven, redeemed, and reconciled to God. The Father patiently *waits* until man is ready and willing to *admit* he needs help.

> *For God so loved the world, that he gave his only begotten Son, that whosoever believeth in him, should not perish but have everlasting life. (John 3:16)*

16. WHAT IS MAN'S GREATEST NEED?

Man needs to be *reconciled* to his Creator. Man needs to find forgiveness for his sins and make peace with his Maker. He needs to *confess* he needs help, that he *cannot* make it on his own. When he has made Jesus Christ the LORD of his life, he will begin to regain the image of God, his lost glory and God-given pride.

> *. . . God was in Christ, reconciling the world unto himself, not imputing their trespasses unto them; and hath committed unto us the word of reconciliation.*
>
> *Now then we are ambassadors for Christ, as though God did beseech you by us; we pray in Christ's stead, be ye reconciled to God.*
> *(2 Cor. 5: 19-20)*
>
> *Let the wicked forsake his way, and the unrighteous man his thoughts; and let him return unto the Lord, and he will have mercy upon him; and to our God, for he will abundantly pardon. (Isa. 55:7)*

Come now, let us reason together, saith the Lord: though your sins be as scarlet, they shall be white as snow; though they be red as crimson, they shall be as wool. (Isa. 1:18)

17. WHAT HINDERS MAN FROM RECONCILING WITH GOD?

Man's ego hinders him from *admitting he was wrong.* Although man is aware something is missing in his life, he unconsciously *fights* having to identify with the fact of *dependence*, to face up to his weakness.

Why do the heathen rage, and the people imagine a vain thing? The kings of the earth set themselves, and the rulers take counsel together, against the LORD, and against his anointed, saying, Let us break their bands asunder, and cast away their cords from us. (Ps. 2:1-3)

18 WHAT IS WRONG WITH MAN PURSUING HIS GOAL AND FULFILLING HIS DREAM?

God has no problem with mankind pursuing his goal, fulfilling his dream. Foolishly, from his beginning, man has turned his back on God and rejected His counsel. He has turned to the "wisdom of this world" and made Satan, God's arch-enemy, his counselor. The results have been devastating and lead to disillusionment and hell.

God did not create man to be a robot, but a unique human being with a free will. Wasn't this risky? Sure, but He wanted man to love Him, submit himself *willingly* to His plan for his life and serve Him with delight.

God *alone* is all-wisdom and all-power. Man is God's creation. He created him to fulfill a *mission*. God alone knows how to instruct man to do it successfully, with satisfaction.

Know ye not, that to whom ye yield yourselves servants to obey, his servants ye are to whom ye obey; whether of sin unto death, or of obedience unto righteousness? (Rom. 6:16)

19. WILL RECONCILIATION WITH GOD AFFECT MAN'S SELF-ESTEEM?

Yes. Man's true self-esteem takes on new value when he is reconciled with God. There is a *marked difference* between man's *self-esteem* and the proud *exaltation of self*, which has rejected God as its only life and power. The scriptures identify **self-exaltation** as the spirit of *Anti-Christ*.

Men are dead to God because they are living to *self*. Without a death to self, there is no escape from Satan's power over them.

And Jesus said to them all, If any man will come

19

*after me, let him **deny himself**, and take up his cross **daily**, and follow me. For whosoever will save his life shall lose it, but whosoever will lose his life for my sake, the same shall save it. For what is a man advantaged, if he gain the whole world, and lose himself, or be cast away?*
(Luke 9: 23-25)

20.   HOW IS MAN RECONCILED TO GOD?

Man's salvation can only be brought about by a reconciling *union* of his spirit with the Spirit of his Creator. We accept God's offer of forgiveness by sincerely asking Him to forgive our *rebellion* against His Lordship, and the breaking of His commandments. We ask His help to seriously build a solid *relationship* with Him.

If we confess our sins, he is faithful and just to forgive us our sins, and to cleanse us from all unrighteousness. (I John 1:9)

A man who refuses to admit his mistakes can never be successful. But if he confesses and forsakes them, he gets another chance. (Prov. 28:13 LB)

21.   HOW DOES GOD HELP US BUILD A SOLID RELATIONSHIP?

The Holy Spirit was sent to earth to woo man back to God. It is the work of the Holy Spirit to *convince* and *enable* man to submit to God's will and deny himself. The Spirit of God gives man the **power of willing**. Man can then will to be what God requires him to be, will to seek no self-ends, but to fill the place and be the person the Creator has ordained.

Henceforth I call you not servants; for the servant knoweth not what his lord doeth: but I have called you friends; for all things that I have heard of my Father I have made known unto you. Ye have not chosen me, but I have chosen you, and ordained you, that ye should go and bring forth fruit, and that your fruit should remain: that whatsoever ye shall ask of the Father in my name, he may give it you. (John 15: 15,16)

22 HOW IS COMPLETE SUBMISSION TO THE WILL OF GOD ACCOMPLISHED?

Complete submission to the will of God can **only** be worked out by the power of the indwelling Holy Spirit, who forms the very life of Christ within the redeemed heart. **The whole nature of virtue consists of *conforming* to the will of God. The whole nature of sin is *rebelling* against it.**

And be not conformed to this world: but be ye transformed by the renewing of your mind, so you may prove what is that good, and perfect, and acceptable will of God. (Rom. 12:2)

23. HOW CAN A MAN BE CHANGED - MADE ANEW?

Man must be *born again*; he needs a *character transplant* to become the person he was meant to be. When a man is born again, the divine nature begins to *develop* in him. This divine life in man is possible because Christ *lives in him*. It is the *indwelling Christ* who produces inner peace, strength and stability that surpasses understanding.

Thank God, we don't need to stay the way we are. The indwelling Lord makes us like Himself which is our highest good, blessing and joy.

> *If any man be in Christ, he is a new creation: old things are passed away: behold, all things are become new. (2 Cor. 5:17)*

24. WHAT IS THE DIVINE NATURE?

The divine nature is *total submission to the Father's will*. It was demonstrated by Jesus Christ as He walked this earth in *agreement* with God. He was totally *submissive* and *obedient* to the Father's plan and will. Because of sin, man has an earthly, sensual and devilish nature. The design of God is to *remove* this earthly nature, make us partakers of the divine nature, and *bring us back* to the image of God.

Then answered Jesus and said unto them, Verily, verily, I say unto you, The Son can do nothing of himself, but what he seeth the Father do: for what things soever he doeth, these also doeth the Son likewise. I can of mine own self do nothing. As I hear, I judge: and my judgment is just; because I seek not mine own will, but the will of the Father which hath sent me. (John 5: 19,30)

*Whereby are given unto us exceeding great and precious promises: that by these ye might be partakers of the **divine nature**, having escaped the corruption that is in the world through lust. (2 Peter 1:4)*

25.   HOW DO WE FIND GOD?

We find God and secure His help when we *earnestly* seek Him through prayer. When we reach out to God for help through prayer, we are acknowledging we *recognize* our weakness and dependence. We show significant spiritual insight when we *admit* the *need* of a relationship with God, in order to become the unique human beings He has created.

And ye shall seek me, and find me, when ye shall search for me with all your heart. (Jer. 29: 13)

26. HOW CAN OUR EARTHLY NATURE BE CHANGED?

The Holy Spirit is the answer. He has come to *indwell us* and *change us*. All that we are to be and do is by the Spirit of Christ living within us. Jesus said, "In that day ye shall know that I am in you." The Spirit of God, living and working in the spirit of man, produces **the spirit of willing**. The Holy Spirit's indwelling gives man power to *submit* to God, *deny* himself and *fulfill* His will.

Christ in you, your hope of glory, is the safe, satisfying, sensible and saving message of the Gospel. I am somebody. I belong to Christ. Therefore, I can do something.

Christ in you, your hope of glory. (Col. 1:27)

I can do all things through Christ which strengtheneth me. (Phil. 4:13)

I am crucified with Christ: nevertheless I live; yet not I, but Christ liveth in me: and the life which I now live in the flesh I live by the faith of the Son of God, who loved me, and gave himself for me. (Gal. 2:20)

*Conformity to
God's will makes
the ordinary actions
of men on earth
an acceptable
service to God.*

CHAPTER THREE

The Miracle Of Pentecost

*But when the Holy Spirit has come upon you, you will
receive power to testify about me with great effect, to the
people in Jerusalem, throughout Judea, in Samaria, and to
the ends of the earth, about my death and resurrection.*
(Acts 1:8 LB)

Although the disciples of Jesus Christ had been
instructed in heavenly truths from Christ
Himself, and enabled to work miracles in His Name,
they were not yet *qualified* to know and teach the *mysteries* of the Kingdom. The real comfort and blessing of
Christ to His followers could only be had through something
more than His physical presence and verbal instruction. His
outward teaching and guidance were to be changed into the
inspiration and operation of His Spirit *resident* in their
souls.

27

When Jesus was with them, in the flesh, He told them it was *absolutely necessary that He go away*. He promised them He would come again in the fullness and power of the Holy Spirit. He would break open the death and darkness of their hearts with light and life from heaven, so they could experience in themselves **all** that He had taught and promised to them.

Jesus commanded them *not* to bear witness to the world what they *humanly knew* of His birth, life, teaching and resurrection. They were to wait in Jerusalem until they were *endued with power* from on High. Only then could the apostles be able ministers, not of the letter, but of the Spirit.

> *For the letter killeth but the Spirit giveth life.*
> (I Cor. 3:6b)

The disciples did not understand His words, but they obeyed Him. One hundred and twenty frightened and discouraged men and women made their way to the Upper Room above a street in Jerusalem where they had eaten the Last Supper with Jesus. After His resurrection, He made several appearances in that room and told them to wait for His return, and that is exactly what they did.

Most likely there was tension in the room. There had been competition among the disciples, criticism of each other. Peter had denied the Lord, Thomas had doubted, and James and John had wrangled over who was the greatest and what position they would have in Jesus' kingdom. Also, there were bad feelings between Jesus' family and the disciples. Jesus had spent His time with a motley band of fishermen, a tax collector, and a zealot with no time for His own family. What about people like Mary Magdalene and others whom the Jews could not tolerate? Jesus healed them from their sins. The disciples were suspicious of this Pharisee Nicodemus. Was he really a disciple? Could he be trusted? And what about rich Joseph of Arimathea?

It was a strange mixture of humanity that gathered in the Upper Room. Each had his or her reason for being there, the knowledge of what Jesus had meant to each of them. But what were they to each other except people who had a common loyalty to Jesus? And He was gone! Now they had to sit and wait . . . look each other in the eye . . . open their hearts to one another . . . share their loneliness, their grief over Jesus' absence and their wonderment about the future.

Jesus said He would be back. Perhaps all was not lost! The anticipation in each of the people in that Upper Room created hope and a bonding together. So what did they do there? They did what Jesus had taught them to do: *they prayed*! Prayer brings unity.

What did they pray about? What could they do to prepare themselves for His coming? The matter of *willingness* surfaced; were they *willing* to leave *all* and follow Him?

Suddenly, a wind began to stir in the room, gently at first, then it grew stronger. The followers of Jesus looked up from their prayers. What was happening? The wind was stronger. Now the wind was rushing with a rumble like thunder...rushing with irresistible force.

The Spirit had filled the room; now He filled the ready disciples and followers **whose preparation had made room for Him**. They were filled to the *full*, they were Spirit-filled, as a vessel is filled.

What the wind does when it rushes, so too the Holy Spirit was doing in their souls. The presence of the wind outwardly was soon an inward rushing of new thought, emotion, and *will*, as it blew out *fear* and *uncertainty*.

Accompanying the wind was *new fire* from heaven that *sat upon each of them*, to burn out anything in them which could cripple them in His service and prevent them from fully becoming the persons they were meant to be.

But the fire of the Holy Spirit did so much more than burn away; He refined and galvanized. The dross was burned off and the pure metal was left. The people in the Upper Room were changed. He had come to *indwell* them and *make them like Himself.* The followers of Christ were being stirred up, quickened, brought back to life because *He* had come.

27. WHAT DID THE "CLOVEN TONGUES OF FIRE" DO TO THEM?

The "cloven tongues of fire" purged their lips as did the live coal off the altar of God used by the angel to touch the lips of the prophet Isaiah.

When the Holy Spirit purges our lips (tongue), He has taken control to use us for His service.

> *And the tongue is a fire, a world of iniquity; so is the tongue among our members, that it defileth the whole body, and setteth on fire the course of nature; and it is set on fire of hell. (Jas. 3:6)*

> *If any man among you seem to be religious, and bridleth not his tongue, but deceiveth his own*

heart, this man's religion is vain. (Jas. 1:26)

Behold also the ships, which though they be so great, and are driven of fierce winds, yet are they turned about with a very small helm, whithersoever the governor listeth. Even so the tongue is a little member, and boasteth great things. Behold, how great a matter a little fire kindleth! (Jas. 3:4-5)

He that hath no rule over his own spirit is like a city that is broken down, and without walls. (Prov. 25:28)

28. WHAT REALLY TOOK PLACE AT PENTECOST?

The followers of Jesus were filled with the Holy Spirit to **praise and proclaim**. The Holy Spirit released them to praise, and that praise became a very effective proclamation. It was the sound of the rushing wind that brought the crowds to the area of the Upper Room, but it was the **quality of praise** that made them want to know what was happening.

. . . we do hear them speak in our tongues the wonderful works of God. And they were all amazed, and were in doubt, saying one to another, What meaneth this? (Acts 2: 11b-12)

29. WHAT WAS THE MIRACLE OF PENTECOST?

Pentecost was the beginning of a new age of spiritual renaissance. **Christ came to *dwell* in redeemed man forever.** What Jesus Christ had tried to explain to His followers had finally happened. There was no other way the followers of Christ could be like-minded with Christ in anything He taught them without His Holy Spirit living within.

God's Spirit produced in His people a *potential* beyond human limitations. What Jesus Christ promised was given to His followers; they became *Christ bearers.*

> *At that day ye shall know that I am in my Father, and **ye in me, and I in you**. (John 14:20)*

> *I will dwell in them, and walk in them; and I will be their God and they shall be my people. (2 Cor. 6:16b)*

> *...Christ in you, the hope of (your) glory (the power of the age to come). (Col. 1:27b)*

30. WHAT DOES IT MEAN TO BE SPIRIT-FILLED?

The followers of Christ were human beings with minds, wills, emotions, and physical bodies. To be filled to the full means the Spirit *invaded* every facet and function of their nature.

31. HOW DOES THE HOLY SPIRIT INVADE MAN'S SPIRIT?

Man's spirit is the port of entry for the divine Spirit. When the Holy Spirit enters a human being, a *miracle* takes place. The mind is transformed, the computer of the brain is given new data, the **will** is released from bondage, and the nervous system becomes the channel of supernatural energy.

I beseech you therefore, brethren, by the mercies of God, that ye present your bodies a living sacrifice, holy, acceptable unto God, which is your reasonable service.

And be not conformed to this world: but be ye transformed by the renewing of your mind, that ye may prove what is that good, and acceptable, and perfect, will of God. (Rom. 12:1,2)

Howbeit when he, the Spirit of truth, is come, he will guide you into all truth . . . (John 16:13a)

32. WHAT DID JESUS CHRIST TEACH ABOUT THE HOLY SPIRIT?

Jesus told Nicodemus he had to be *born again* of the Spirit to enter the Kingdom of God. He explained to the woman of Samaria: **God is Spirit.** Jesus Christ explained the higher law of *transformation* in His life and message: our spirit can be infused and empowered by the Holy Spirit. **We were created for Spirit-to-spirit union and communication.**

God is a Spirit: and they that worship him must worship him in spirit and in truth. (John 4:24)

33. DID THE DISCIPLES KNOW HOW CHRIST WOULD EMPOWER THEM?

No. The final hours before Pentecost were filled with the anxious frustration of the impossibility of *living*

Christ's message and emulating His life. How could this happen without Him? Although He had clearly said He would come and **make His home in them, they had not realized what He meant.**

The disciples waited on the edge of a miracle, **history's greatest miracle: "the transformation of human personality and the beginning of a new humanity."** (Lloyd Ogilive) They were to be men and women **in Jesus Christ** and *He would dwell in them.*

> *Christ in you, the hope of glory. (Col. 1:27)*

> *At that day (Pentecost) ye shall know that I am in my Father and ye in me and I in you. (John 14:20)*

34. DOES THE INDWELLING SPIRIT CHANGE US?

Yes. It is a miracle! A personality is *transformed*, a person is able to think or act beyond the limitations of his or her capacities. A higher power, exercising a higher law, multiplies the human potential.

The miracle of a *changed personality* results in supernatural gifts of intellect, emotional freedom and a conviction that all things are possible. The word "impossible" no longer has its restricting confinement. The impossible happens.

> *Therefore if any man be in Christ, he is a new creature: old things are passed away; behold, all things are become new. (2 Cor. 5:17)*

For in Christ Jesus neither circumcision availeth anything, nor uncircumcision, but a new creature. (Gal. 6:15)

35. HOW DID THE DISCIPLES KNOW THEY HAD RECEIVED THE GIFT OF THE HOLY SPIRIT?

A **praising tongue** was the undeniable evidence. The followers of the Master were *ecstatic with praise.* Galileans, whose language was Aramic, were able to speak Latin, Greek and all other languages represented by the people gathered from around the known world. The mighty, rushing wind had stimulated their minds, and the fire had kindled their emotions. They both thought and felt *uncontainable adoration.* A miracle had occurred: they were able to speak in languages they *never learned* and were understood.

The evidence of the filling of the Holy Spirit is a freedom from self-concern to Spirit-consciousness. We are released to praise God with unfettered joy and gratitude.

And they were all amazed and marveled, saying to one another, Look, are not all these who speak Galilean? And how is it we hear, each in our own language in which we were born? ...We hear them speaking in our tongues the wonderful works of God. (Acts 2:7-8,11 NKJ)

36. WHAT ABOUT THE GIFT OF OTHER TONGUES?

Luke tells us that **the praise** of the Spirit-filled believers was spoken in the languages of the people gathered in Jerusalem. This is an indication of how completely **filled** and under the influence of the Spirit they were. The magnificent mechanism of speech was utilized by Him to enable the believers to think and articulate in languages they had not previously learned.

Whenever the Holy Spirit's power fell on believers, listeners heard them *praise* God with tongues and prophecy. Tongues is a sign that *follows* those who believe. Regretfully, many believers seek "tongues" rather than to be a *praise giver* who witnesses God's goodness and mercy in the earth.

37. WHY IS A PRAISING "OTHER" TONGUE THE EVIDENCE OF THE SPIRIT'S INDWELLING?

Praise is the secret of the liberated life. There is a *power in praise* that needs to be discovered by the people to whom we communicate. Praising the Lord for what He has done frees us to receive what He will do. But also, praise is the ultimate key to human relinquishment of our *will* to the Lord. When we praise Him for problems or unresolved tensions, we release them to Him in an unreserved way that *frees* us from the grip of anxiety.

The praise of the newly filled believers was what caused the crowd to gather that day in Jerusalem. It was not just that they heard in their own language, but **what** they heard that was so astonishing. The desire to *praise* lies deep within every human being. The praise the crowd heard for what the Lord was doing touched a resounding chord within them. When we *hear* authentic praise, we are drawn mysteriously, irrevocably.

38. WHAT IS THE DIFFERENCE BETWEEN "OTHER TONGUES" AND THE GIFT OF TONGUES?

It is important to distinguish between "other tongues" and the gift of tongues. At Pentecost, for the 120 to speak in the languages of the different nationalities was a miracle of communication.

Later in the development of the Church, the Holy Spirit gave a *gift of utterance* which was *not* a specific language. Rather, words and sounds were given by the Spirit to release the believers *for praise* beyond the capacity of expression in the words of their own languages, and also for prophesies to the Church.

Other tongues accompany the Baptism of the Holy Spirit and spirit prayer. The gift of "tongues" is accompanied by the gift of "interpretation of tongues".

Even so ye, forasmuch as ye are zealous of spiritual gifts, seek that ye may excel to the edifying of the church. Wherefore let him that speaketh in an unknown tongue pray that he may interpret. For if I pray in an unknown tongue, my spirit prayeth, but my understanding is unfruitful. (I Cor. 14:12-14)

*These **signs** shall follow them that believe . . . they shall speak with new tongues. (Mark 16:17)*

39.   WHAT IS SPIRIT PRAYER?

When the Holy Spirit came, He opened a new and direct channel of communication to the Father, who is Spirit. Spirit Prayer is the enablement to communicate directly with God by praying in an unknown tongue.

> *For we don't even know what we should pray for as we should: but the Holy Spirit prays for us with such feeling that it cannot be expressed in words.*

> *And the Father who knows all hearts knows, of course, what the Spirit is saying as he pleads for us in harmony with God's own will. (Rom. 8:26-27 LB)*

> *For he that speaketh in an unknown tongue speaketh not unto men <u>but unto God</u>. (I Cor. 14:2)*

40.   WHAT WILL MAKE OUR LIFE A PRAISE TO GOD?

Outward professions of allegiance to Christ often cover a rebellious heart. Complete submission to the will of God can only be worked out by the power of the indwelling Holy Spirit, forming the very life of Christ within the redeemed heart. **It is the willing and obedient, the totally devoted whose life is a praise to God.**

41.   WHAT WAS THE PURPOSE OF THE HOLY SPIRIT COMING?

All types and shadows in the Old Testament were but empty shadows without the coming of Jesus Christ. In like manner, the New Testament is but dead letter without the Holy Spirit residing in redeemed man as the living power of a full salvation.

The New Testament without the coming of the Holy Spirit in *power over self, sin and the devil*, is no better a help to man to reach heaven than the Old Testament without the coming of the Messiah.

CHAPTER FOUR

A New Heart And A New Spirit

I will give you a new heart, and put a new spirit within
you; I will take the heart of stone out of your flesh and
give you a heart of flesh. (Ezekiel 36:26 NKJ)

A few years after I had received the gift of the Spirit, the indwelling Holy Spirit began the purifying and refining work Jesus Christ promised He would do in me. I was convicted of *my* stubborn, rebellious heart. In the beginning, I resisted the Spirit's probes and made excuses for my behavior as something that was a part of my personality.

I felt comfortable with that explanation, and for a time it seemed to sooth my conscience. That is, until a prayer meeting was started at our local church on Monday nights, and I was asked to be the leader. Fear gripped me. I had a strong intuitive feeling where this prayer meeting would lead me. My deepest fears would be realized, and I would end up becoming a preacher like my mother. I had seen, firsthand, the persecution my mother received as a woman in the ministry. I was determined this would never happen to me.

The following month, our local church had its annual fall convention. One of the guest speakers was an old-time family friend from California. He greeted me in the dining area with a pat on the back as he inquired, "How is my friend, Preacher Pat?" His greeting pushed the right button. It rattled the cage of every spirit of rebellion and fear that tormented me. They stood up to be counted. I do not recall my retort, but my reddened face exposed my heart. I returned home defeated.

It was winter and the snow was deep, with the temperature hovering near zero. The Monday Night Prayer Group, of which my husband, Peter, and I were leaders, requested an opportunity to gain experience in leading church services. We were excited when a small church in Cottom, Ontario extended an invitation to us to help them with their Sunday evening services. Our pastor agreed and let us use an old Sunday School bus for transportation. That was great, until we discovered the heater in the bus did not work.

Twenty-four eager, amateur revivalists, with musical instruments, blankets and Bibles, made the 76 mile trip from Detroit, Michigan across the Canadian border to Cottom, Ontario every Sunday evening throughout those bitter-cold winter months.

Our Canadian friends were happy to see that old bus pull up to the church door every Sunday evening; we almost filled the church. They were so friendly, gracious and patient with our amateur performance and encouraged us by responding to the Word. Evidently, the Holy Spirit was pleased too, for He was there in attendance to work in the hearts of the people, especially the amateur revivalists.

I cannot recall who preached or what was preached, but on one particular Sunday evening, old-fashioned conviction gripped my heart. Godly sorrow for my sin of *persistent resistance* and *rebellion* against God's rule and will in my life swept over my soul like a tidal wave; I could not stop weeping. *The vital necessity of placing myself completely under the power and control of the Holy Spirit, both for salvation and my eternal well-being, allowing Him to live through me the very purpose for which God created me, was made so real to me.* I recall many, *many* days of deep repentance and also the frightening times, when I honestly did not see how He could forgive me.

The Monday Night Prayer Group was made up of adults from 20 to 40 years of age. Most of them were from Christian homes, raised in the church. Faith in God was professed with their lips, but they had never experienced old-time religion's heart-searching conviction and repentance for sin. Christianity is a *revealed* religion, not a *natural* (man-made) religion. They were good people, but had never become **new creatures in Christ Jesus**.

The Monday gatherings turned into an "Old Time Religion" soul-searching, repenting, God-seeking prayer meeting to know and understand God's will. It was in one of these meetings the Holy Spirit spoke these words emphatically to my spirit, "What you need is a circumcised heart!"

I could not recall ever hearing those words before, but those words were *burned* into my heart. Somehow I knew *those words were to change my life forever*.

When we rose from prayer, I shared what I had heard with the group. We took our Bibles and began to search the Scriptures for a definition and an understanding of these power-packed words. We discovered a *circumcised heart* was clearly related to a biblical covenant.

42. WHAT IS A BIBLICAL COVENANT?

One of the words most used in scripture is *covenant*. It is impossible to understand the Bible without understanding the meaning of this word. A *covenant* is a solemn agreement between two or more parties. It involves a formal statement of the rights and responsibilities between those involved.

We have very few examples left of *covenant* in modern society. Marriage is the best example that comes to mind. In a marriage, the man and woman solemnly vow to remain with one another "in sickness and in health, for richer and for poorer, for better and for worse." They evoke the name of God. They exchange rings. They light the unity candle. They sign state documents. Even with the decay of marriage in our times, it is still a complicated process to dissolve its entanglements. Biblical covenants are very much like that.

43. WHAT WAS THE PURPOSE OF A COVENANT?

After God had destroyed the world with a flood and saved Noah and his family, the peoples of the earth again became numerous. Unfortunately, all human beings who survived were still infected with sin. The human race continued in moral decline even though evil had already led to it's near annihilation.

As the Lord looked upon the peoples of the earth, He found the man Abram, who lived in Ur of the Chaldeans, with whom He could make a *covenant*. Abraham was a man who would be obedient to His commands and in turn God would bless him. He would become the Father of a *covenant* family, a family that would "pass down" *righteousness and truth* - even as others passed down iniquity and unbelief. Abraham's faith prompted him "to go out into a place which he should after receive for an inheritance." (Heb. 11:8) His faith produced *obedience*. He "went out not knowing whither he went."

44. WHAT WAS THE SIGN OF THE SEAL OF GOD'S COVENANT WITH ABRAHAM?

The seal of God's covenant with Abraham and his family was the circumcision of Hebrew males. This involved a mark of separation in the very flesh of the Hebrew men, a visible reminder that they were not to be as other people.

The subject of *circumcision* as a religious rite seems rather strange to us today. It is, however, a prominent subject in Holy Scripture. There seems to have been several reasons for the use of circumcision as a covenant rite. But for whatever reason, the male Israelite carried a sign in his very body that said to both himself and to the practitioners of heathen religions - religions which used sex rituals in their worship practices - "this man is in covenant with Jehovah." To be a Hebrew was to be different.

45. WHAT CAUSED THE OLD COVENANT TO BE ABOLISHED?

The Lord kept His covenant promises to bless, multiply, prosper and protect the nation of Israel, but they *did not* keep their covenant agreement with Him. They disobeyed Jehovah's commandments, intermarried with the heathen, and refused to be led by His Spirit. When the terms of the covenant were broken *repeatedly*, from generation to generation, the first or old covenant was abolished.

46. DID GOD FORSAKE ISRAEL?

No. He spoke through His prophet Moses.

> *The Lord your God will circumcise your heart and the heart of your descendants, to love the Lord...*
> *(Deut. 30:6 NKJ)*

Moses realized that in Israel's present state, the people could never love God enough to remain obedient to the law; **there must be a change of heart**. God promised He would replace Israel's former spiritual insensitivity and stubbornness with a new will to obey him.

The prophet Ezekiel also prophesied God would make a new and different *covenant* with the house of Israel.

*I will **give you a new heart and put a new spirit within you**; I will take the heart of stone out of your flesh and give you a heart of flesh. I will put My spirit within you and cause you to walk in My statutes, and you will **keep my judgments and do them**. (Eze 36: 26-27 NKJ)*

47. WHAT IS A CIRCUMCISED HEART?

The term "circumcised heart" is recorded in the Bible in many prophetic statements by Old Testament Prophets such as Moses and Jeremiah. If the heart is *circumcised*, then that which *hinders obedience* to God is *cut* away, and it becomes open and free from *obstructions*. Man's innate desire to be *independent* of God's control is gone. The result of such a circumcision will be *submission* to the will of God and the *end* of stubbornness.

Therefore circumcise the foreskin of your heart, and be stiff-necked no longer. (Deut. 10:16 NKJ)

I delight to do thy will, O my God: yea, thy law is within my heart. (Ps. 40:8)

48. WHAT IS THE NEW COVENANT?

The New Covenant is a love relationship with our God. The promises made to Abraham in the old covenant are now given to the people of God, who have made an everlasting *covenant* with their Lord and Master.

Jesus Christ established a new covenant with His Father by laying down His life for us. His own precious blood was shed on Calvary's cross for the sins of the world. He made peace with God so we could be *reconciled* to Him and enjoy personal, intimate fellowship with our Creator.

Behold, the days are coming, says the Lord, when I will make a new covenant with the house of Israel and with the house of Judah - not according to the covenant that I made with their fathers in the day that I took them by the hand to lead them out of the land of Egypt, My covenant which they broke, though I was a husband to them, says the Lord. But this is the covenant that I will make with the house of Israel after those days, says the Lord: I will put My law in their minds, and write it on their hearts; and I will be their God, and they shall be My people. No more shall every man teach his neighbor, and every man his brother, saying, 'Know the

Lord,' for they all shall know Me, from the least of them to the greatest of them, says the Lord. For I will forgive their iniquity, and their sin I will remember no more. (Jer.31: 31-34 NKJ)

49. DID JESUS CHRIST TEACH THAT MAN NEEDED A NEW HEART AND A NEW SPIRIT?

Yes. Jesus told Nicodemus, a ruler of the Jews, that he must be *born again*. He could not see or enter the Kingdom of God unless he had a new birth of water and Spirit.

Jesus answered and said unto him, Verily, verily, I say unto thee, Except a man be born again, he cannot see the kingdom of God.

Jesus answered, Verily, verily, I say unto thee, Except a man be born of water and of the Spirit, he cannot enter into the kingdom of God. That which is born of the flesh is flesh; and that which is born of the Spirit is spirit. Marvel not that I said unto thee, Ye must be born again. (John 3: 3,5-7)

50. WHAT IS THE SEAL OF THE NEW COVENANT?

Believing men and women are circumcised in heart when they are *baptized* into Christ. A Christian baptism is not unlike Jewish circumcision. Paul says **that**

in baptism we are marked as *Christians*. This is a circumcision made without hands, the circumcision of Christ in which we are *"buried with Him in baptism."*

The change from the rite of *circumcision* in the Old Covenant, to *baptism* in the New Covenant, was made easier by the fact that women converts had long been baptized for *initiation* into Judaism. It would not have sounded strange to first century believers to hear St. Paul assure them in Col. 2:12 that *baptism* is a *"true circumcision"* or one that does in fact what the old physical mark merely symbolized: it *circumcises the heart.*

> *For in Him dwelleth all the fullness of the Godhead bodily. And ye are complete in Him, which is the head of all principality and power:*
>
> *In whom ye also are circumcised with the circumcision made without hands, in putting off the body of the sins of the flesh by the circumcision of Christ:*
>
> *Buried with him in baptism, wherein also ye are risen with him through the faith of the operation of God, who hath raised him from the dead.*
>
> *And you, being dead in your sins and the uncircumcision of your flesh, hath he quickened together with him, having forgiven you all trespasses. (Col. 2: 9-13)*

51. WHAT HAPPENS TO A BELIEVER'S HEART?

The Spirit of God removes the stony heart of *rebellion* and *unbelief* in an operation made without human hands. A new heart and a new spirit is given to the believer, a heart that loves God and serves Him *willingly*.

> *Know ye not, that so many of us as were baptized into Jesus Christ were baptized into his death? (Rom. 6:3)*

> *For as many of you as have been baptized into Christ have put on Christ. (Gal.3:27)*

> *And you hath he quickened, who were dead in trespasses and sins; (Eph. 2:1)*

52. DO WE TRULY WALK IN NEWNESS OF LIFE?

Yes. It is true, old things pass away and **all things** become new. Our lifestyle, our conversation, and our ambitions are turned **from self to pleasing God**.

> *I am crucified with Christ: nevertheless I live; yet not I, but Christ liveth in me: and the life which I now live in the flesh I live by the faith of the Son of God, who loved me, and gave himself for me. (Gal. 2:20)*

53. WHAT HAPPENED TO THE MONDAY NIGHT PRAYER GROUP?

When the students really understood there is nothing *wise*, or *holy*, or *just* except the perfect will of God, they wholeheartedly sought the Lord that He would *circumcise* their hearts.

The results of the spiritual operation of God upon their hearts were astounding. Conformity to God's will makes the ordinary actions of men upon earth an *acceptable* service to God. They became truly connected to the True Vine, and His life began to flow through them. As they abode in the Vine and He in them, they brought forth *much* fruit.

The Monday Night Prayer Meeting became the Minister Candidate School. When the students had completed three years together, they graduated to take their place of ministry in His service. Over the next twenty-three years, pastors, missionaries, church leaders, Bible study leaders, church school teachers, small group facilitators, and many faithful individual Christians were the precious fruit of the MCS classes.

*When someone becomes a Christian he becomes a brand new person inside. He is **not the same any more**. A new life has begun! (2 Cor. 5:17 LB)*

Everybody wants a personal testimony of the miracle working power of God, but nobody wants a test to produce it.

CHAPTER FIVE

The Testing Of Our Faith

But he knoweth the way that I take:
When he hath tried me, I shall come forth as gold.
(Job 23:10)

I t has been said, *Everybody wants a personal testimony of the miracle working power of God, but nobody wants a test to produce it.* The idea that God might initiate a test is foreign to many people both outside and inside the Kingdom. Modern man, if he believes in God, has a tendency to think of the God in whom he believes as a *benevolent* figure, whose main concern is to make man feel good about himself. This God is regarded as something like the recreational director on a cruise ship, whose task is to give everyone a good time, with no expense spared.

But the Apostle James put it in perspective when he wrote,

My brethren, count it all joy when you fall into various trials, knowing that the testing of your faith produces patience. But let patience have its perfect work, that you may be perfect and complete, lacking nothing. (Jas 1:2-4 NKJ)

Faith is matured through the experience of stressful *testing* in much the same way that the cardiovascular system is strengthened through exercise and the muscles are developed by pumping iron. The Apostle James made another major contribution to our understanding. He used Abraham's sacrificial offering of his son, Isaac at Mt. Moriah as an example. He explained, *Faith by itself, if it does not have works, is dead. (James 2:17 NKJ)*

Classic illustrations of such testings are found in the Bible stories of God testing Joseph, Job, Daniel and the Hebrew children. They all remained true to God, even in the time of danger and suffering. Daniel and the Hebrew children even refused to worship a Babylonian god, though it meant the lion's den or a fiery furnace.

Such testing is a necessary part of life in revealing the true *mettle* of a man. It is through severe testing that a man or woman's true courage or strength of character is revealed.

There is an old Jewish saying, "The Holy One, blest be His name, does not elevate a man to dignity until He has first tried and searched him; if he stands in temptation then He raises him to dignity."

THE TESTING OF CHRIST

Similarly, the testing of Jesus is the demonstration of His full commitment to His Father's will. Jesus had His sense of vocation tested with the choice between God's Kingdom and Satan's. The devil was an agent in the testing; the choice was as much *to rise* as *to fall*.

Jesus Christ came to earth to redeem mankind from the curse of the Fall, the slavery of Satan, and the power of sin. But in order to accomplish this, He must first be tested and tried as a man. Adam's sin was a calculated denial of God's authority and a clear statement of his intention to go his own way. What would this second Adam do? Would He accomplish the will of the Father or go His own way?

When Jesus Christ was baptized in the Jordan River by His cousin, John the Baptist, He was empowered by the descending Holy Spirit. The Voice of the Father was heard from heaven declaring, *"This is My beloved Son, in whom I am well pleased!"* Immediately afterward, the Holy Spirit drove him by force into the wilderness, where He would be tested and subjected to a merciless attack on His body, soul and spirit by Lucifer, the devil himself.

If there were any hidden character weaknesses to *incite rebellion and independence* in Jesus Christ, Satan had a free hand to find and expose them. This was his once-in-a-life-time opportunity.

About thirty miles away from the Jordan River, where Jesus had been baptized by John, was a large wilderness area of jagged and warped landscape. The hills to the south ran right out to the edge of the Dead Sea, dropping down 1200 feet into the lowest spot on earth. Here in this wilderness area, with intense heat and emptiness, Jesus spent forty days without food, wrestling with the issues in His calling to messianic ministry and the methods He should use to *fulfill* this task.

Jesus knew He *must* drink the cup which held the wrath of God upon the world's sin: the *horror* of the cross. When His body was weakened and His resistance totally undermined from hunger, sleepless nights, and mental harassment, He was attacked by the devil with the *enormity* of his task: the great *suffering* and agonizing *death* He would endure.

While Jesus was in this weakened, vulnerable condition, Lucifer tempted Him with the *alternate* ways of escape to achieve His goal. Why should He die so young when there was another route He could take to win the world? Do it *your* way Jesus, *rebel*! Why choose suffering and death on a cross?

The tempter attacked Jesus Christ from three different angles:

> Become an **economic Messiah**. Use your powers - command these stones to be bread.

> Become a wonder-worker, a miraculously **introduced national leader**. Throw yourself down and let the angels catch you - attract people to follow you.

> **Avoid the cross - take another route.** Worship me! I will give you the kingdoms of the world.

We can never understand or appreciate the *intensity* of Christ's temptation, for the strength of all temptation *terminates* at the moment we surrender. Jesus is the only person who truly knows the *full weight* of temptation, in that He is the *only person* who **never** surrendered or yielded Himself to the temptation of Satan. Jesus' victory over the tempter is our basis for victory as disciples of Jesus Christ.

> *This High Priest of ours understands our weakness-*
> *es, since he had the same temptations we do, though*
> *he never once gave way to them and sinned. So let*
> *us come boldly to the very throne of God and stay*
> *there to receive his mercy and to find grace to help*
> *us in our times of need. (Heb. 4: 15-16 LB)*

54. WHAT IS GOD'S PURPOSE FOR TESTING US?

God tests His sons and daughters primarily to *show* them what is in their heart and to *strengthen* and *perfect* their faith in Him.

> *And thou shalt remember all the way which the*
> *Lord thy God led thee these forty years in the*
> *wilderness, to humble thee, and to prove (test) thee,*
> *to know what was in thine heart, whether thou*
> *wouldest keep his commandments, or no.*
> *(Deut.8:2)*

55. IS TESTING THE SAME AS "THE BAPTISM OF FIRE"?

There is no clear explanation in the scriptures to define the baptism of fire. When the intensity of the testing is *severe, however*, we have reason to believe it is a *baptism of fire*. The Bible commentators refer to the crucifixion of Jesus, the persecution of the early church, and the martyrdom of John as a baptism of fire.

Jesus said that He came to *send fire* on the earth rather than *peace*, and a man's foes would be of his own household. (Luke 12:49) also (Matt 10:36) That's fire!

After His ascension, Jesus Christ sent the Holy Spirit to earth to indwell us. The Holy Spirit's presence *convicts* us of sin and *convinces* us of righteousness, *reveals* truth, *guides* our life, and *tests* the strength and quality of our faith. The Holy Ghost fire refines, purifies and consumes anything that hinders our maturity and progress.

> *. . . He shall baptize you with the Holy Spirit and with fire. He will separate the chaff from the grain, burning the chaff with never-ending fire, and storing away the grain. (Matt. 3:11b-12 LB)*

> *Let God train you, for he is doing what any loving father does for his children. Whoever heard of a son who was never corrected? If God doesn't punish you when you need it, as other fathers punish their sons, then it means that you aren't really God's son at all - that you don't really belong in his family. Since we respect our fathers here on earth, though they punish us, should we not all the more cheerfully submit to God's training so that we can begin really to live?*

> *Our earthly fathers trained us for a few brief years, doing the best for us that they knew how, but God's*

*correction is always right and for the best good,
that we may* **share his holiness***. Being punished
isn't enjoyable while it is happening - it hurts! But
afterwards we can see* **the result, a quiet growth in
grace and character***. (Heb. 12:7-11 LB)*

56. WHY DO WE STILL HAVE PROBLEMS WITH OUR SINFUL NATURE?

Some people have assumed that the "old man" is the
sinful nature, which because the Bible says has been
crucified, must be dead and therefore no longer oper-
ative.

When confronted with the obvious truth: *It may be
dead but it won't lie down*, they have tried to make
their theology fit their experience or vice versa. They
have resorted to many unsatisfactory methods which
have often produced results such as nervous break-
downs or blatant hypocrisy.

We should **not** assume that the *"old man"* is anything
more than *"the man of old"* or the *pre-regenerate person*. The person you were *before Christ* has been
judged, condemned, sentenced, executed, buried and
finished *forever*. The *new man* lives.

Redeemed mankind is no longer totally at the mercy
of the *inhospitable environment of sin*, but is **alive** to
all the power and life of God Himself.

> ... seeing that ye have put off the old man with his
> deeds; (Col.3:9)

57. CAN WE HAVE VICTORY OVER SIN?

Most certainly! The believer must make some decisions *not to let* sin reign in *his* mortal body. There is
nothing very mysterious about this instruction. It
means saying **"no"** in no uncertain terms! Whenever
a believer **obeys the passions of his body and suc-
cumbs to temptation, he sins.** But he is not obligat-
ed to succumb and he does not have to sin.

> *Likewise reckon ye also yourselves to be dead
> indeed unto sin, but alive unto God through Jesus
> Christ our Lord. (Rom. 6:11)*

58. WHY DO WE FIND IT SO DIFFICULT TO
LIVE HOLY LIVES?

Habits are very hard to break. The habits we developed in our former sinful life need to be broken. This
is difficult, but certainly *not* impossible. God does
not take away our ability to sin; He gives us the power
not to sin.

59. WHY DO WE SIN?

Sin is a willful act of disobedience. It is a blatant dis-
play of an independent spirit. We sin when we *yield*
or *present* our tongue to say the wrong word, our hand

to take something that does not belong to us, our sexual organs to commit sexual sins, and our minds to harbor uncharitable thoughts.

When we take sin seriously, we begin to see how sin cannot operate in our bodies without our *giving over* a particular member of the body for a specific sin. If the believer is adequately aware of this, he can begin to say **"no!"** to a temptation, not only in a general sense, but in the *very specific sense* of refusing to present the ***member*** necessary for the committing of sin.

What then? Shall we sin because we are not under law but under grace? Certainly not!

Do you not know that to whom you present yourselves slaves to obey, you are that one's slaves whom you obey, whether of sin leading to death, or of obedience leading to righteousness?

I speak in human terms because of the weakness of your flesh. For just as you presented your members as slaves of uncleanness, and of lawlessness leading to more lawlessness, so now present your members as slaves of righteousness for holiness.
(Rom. 6: 15-16, 19 NKJ)

60. WHAT SHOULD WE DO WHEN WE FALL?

When you sin, the Holy Spirit will *convict* you. Don't ignore the conviction. Acknowledge your guilt and ask for forgiveness. When we confess our failure and sins to Jesus Christ, our great high-priest who knows the weaknesses of our flesh, He will forgive us and help us to understand *why* we succumbed to temptation so we can overcome our weakness. But it is most important that we **acknowledge the truth**. **That is the key.** Don't blame anyone else. Remember Esau, who would not acknowledge his guilt and never found forgiveness.

> *If we confess our sins, He (Jesus) is faithful and just to forgive us our sins and to cleanse us from all unrighteousness. (1 John 1:9 NKJ)*

> *In humility correcting those who are in opposition, if God perhaps will grant them repentance, so that they may know the truth, and that they may come to their senses and escape the snare of the devil, having been taken captive by him to do his will. (2 Tim. 2: 25,26 NKJ)*

61. HOW CAN WE LIVE ABOVE SIN?

If we live and walk **daily** with the Holy Spirit, we will not sin. The believer must *mind* the things of the Spirit rather than those of the flesh. He must choose to *walk* according to the Spirit and **do the right things** rather than *walk* according to the flesh. He is required through the Spirit to put to death the deeds of the body.

Therefore, brethren, we are debtors - not to the flesh, to live according to the flesh.

For if you live according to the flesh you will die; but if by the Spirit you put to death the deeds of the body, you will live. (Rom. 8: 12-13 NKJ)

62. ARE TRIALS PROOF OF GOD'S LOVE FOR US?

Most definitely. The true purpose for trials is **to make us holy people**. Without trials, we will never understand ourselves and our weaknesses. We learn God and His ways when we go through trials and learn to appreciate His presence and power to deliver us.

. . . for he that hath suffered in the flesh hath ceased from sin; (I Peter 4:1b)

So, get your life on track with God, get rid of your old habits, change your lifestyle. It's important! Remember, without holiness you cannot see God.

Wherefore lift up the hands which hang down, and the feeble knees; And make straight paths for your feet, lest that which is lame be turned out of the way; but let it rather be healed. Follow peace with all men, and holiness, without which no man shall see the Lord: (Heb.12:12-14)

63. HOW DOES GOD WANT US TO REGARD TESTINGS?

God wants us to *grow up* and *mature* until we regard ***testings as a new adventure***. As we pass through the many trials and testings of life, we look back at our testimonies of God's great interventions in our life. We remember the times He healed us or delivered us from an impossible situation. As we reflect on the past blessings of our life, we encourage ourselves in the Lord. When a new testing comes our way, we can't help but wonder what great lessons of faith and trust we will learn this time. We have learned by past experiences that another great miracle of God's intervention is awaiting us. We rejoice in the testing of our faith, knowing a great blessing awaits us again.

My brethren, count it all joy when ye fall into divers temptations; Knowing this, that the trying of your faith worketh patience. (Jas 1:2,3)

That the trial of your faith, being much more precious than of gold that perisheth, though it be tried with fire, might be found unto praise and honour and glory at the appearing of Jesus Christ: (1Pet.1:7)

*Forgiveness is
never easy.*

CHAPTER SIX

Freedom Through Forgiveness

. . .Bring out the prisoners from the prison, and them that sit in darkness out of the prison house.
(Isa. 42:7)

*T*he Gospel of Matthew records Jesus Christ's best known sermons, *The Sermon on the Mount* and *The Beatitudes.* Jesus had withdrawn from the crowds to a setting on the mountainside somewhere near the Sea of Galilee. *When He was seated, He opened His mouth and taught them.* His teachings called for a *change* in the thinking of His followers about the Kingdom of God, a rejecting of their popular messianic expectations. He laid out a new lifestyle for the "new creation", citizens of the Kingdom of God, who are born of the Spirit.

Jesus' teachings were revolutionary: love for enemies rather than hate, unconditional forgiveness rather than retaliation, long suffering rather than impatience, and blessing for peacemakers instead of hymns of hate and revenge.

Christ bestowed a **blessing** upon the poor in spirit - the humble - those in poverty of spirit, who were solely dependent upon God. **You are blessed** if you care deeply enough to mourn. **You are blessed** if you possess a gentle, meek spirit that is disciplined and controlled by the Holy Spirit. **You are blessed** if you hunger and thirst for more of God; you shall be filled. **You are blessed if you are merciful**, *for you shall obtain mercy.*

He shocked them with His teaching: **Love your enemies, bless those who curse you, forgive men their trespasses and you will be forgiven**. One who *truly understands God's mercy* and the freedom of being forgiven will share the same release with others. On the other hand, one who refuses to forgive breaks down the bridge over which he himself would pass.

> *He shall have judgment without mercy, that hath shewed no mercy. (Jas 2:13)*

TAKE A GOOD LOOK AT FORGIVENESS

It has been said, "To err is human, to forgive is divine." Forgiveness is *never* easy. It is the most difficult thing in the universe. Forgiveness means that the forgiving person, even though he be the innocent one, willingly resolves his anger over the sin of the guilty one and lets the guilty one **go free**.

To forgive proves one *genuinely* loves and can move beyond the offense to the person. It means one cares more about the person than about what he or she has done. Forgiveness liberates. Forgiveness frees the person for the

70

options of living.

Human nature is inclined to resent rather than to release, to demand rather than to forgive. Our refusal to forgive is a power-play that limits the offender, that holds the guilty "under one's thumb, (or power)." Forgiveness takes the place of revenge. The problem is **we cannot be forgiven if we do not forgive from the heart**.

64. WHAT IS MEANT BY "FREEDOM THROUGH FORGIVENESS"?

You can be free from unresolved anger that eats at your heart like a festering, untreated wound and robs your life of joy. You **can experience through forgiveness**: glorious freedom, deep inner-peace, freedom from anger and rage, deliverance from depression and destructive self-depreciation.

65. ARE MEN AND WOMEN HELD PRISONER BY UNFORGIVENESS?

Yes. At some time, we all have suffered from false accusations, unjustified criticism, harsh judgment, withheld honors, deferred credits, unreturned friendship, neglected recognition, inadequate compensation, physical or emotional neglect, betrayed confidences, and unrequited love . . . to name a few.

Everyone deserves to enjoy a healthy, happy, good life. Unfortunately, early in life we discover we *cannot* have life without hurts; we are all victims of life's injustices. Too often these unresolved, untreated wounds are allowed to fester for years and become emotional cancers that *destroy* our quality of life and *lock* us into a prison of inner rage and self-deprecation.

Whatever (offense) you bind on earth will be bound in heaven, and whatever (hurts, anger, resentment) you loose (forgive and release) on earth will be loosed in heaven. (Matt. 18:18 NKJ)

66. WHAT DOES TRUE FORGIVENESS REALLY INVOLVE?

Forgiveness is giving up your *resentment* against an offender. It is turning aside from the desire to punish and to seek revenge. It is canceling a debt by pardoning the offense. Forgiveness is an act of our will. We can truly forgive when we **will** to forgive.

When ye stand praying, forgive, if ye have ought against any: that your Father also which is in heaven may forgive you your trespasses. (Mark 11:25)

67. HOW DO YOU IDENTIFY AN OFFENDER?

An offender is anyone who uses his power to *hurt* instead of *heal*. We have all been victims and we have all been offenders at some time. We *all* make mistakes.

68. WHO IS REALLY ABLE TO FORGIVE AN OFFENDER?

You can, when you have experienced God's forgiveness. Forgiveness is where we run face to face with God's goodness. It is not easy. Life is made up of decisions, and decisions reveal a man's inner nature.

Forgiving is probably the **hardest task** we may face in our lifetime. Yet the alternative is unthinkable, a life filled with bitterness, hate and anger. Contrary to popular thought, there is nothing *sweet* about revenge.

> *But if ye do not forgive, neither will your Father which is in heaven forgive your trespasses. (Mark 11:26)*

69. HOW IS REAL FORGIVENESS POSSIBLE?

You will receive what you need to forgive an offender by believing on the Lord Jesus Christ. He will give you the *power* you need to forgive your enemies.

You need to be encouraged. You need emotional nourishment. You will find it by understanding that Christianity is a religion based on *mercy* and rooted in *forgiveness*. Christianity is the only religion that accepts *grace* as its source of salvation, not good works.

If you want to keep from becoming fainthearted and

weary, think about his (Jesus') patience as sinful men did such terrible things to him. (Heb.12:3 LB)

Neither do I condemn thee: go and sin no more. (John 8:11)

70. IS IT POSSIBLE TO TRULY FORGIVE?

Yes. Forgiveness is impossible on your own, but with God's help it is *possible* to forgive those who have hurt you. We know we have *truly forgiven* when the *sting* of the offense is gone and the wound has healed.

I can do all things through Christ who strengtheneth me. (Phil. 4:13)

71. HOW CAN WE BE SURE FORGIVENESS WILL WORK FOR US?

Jesus Christ has given us His Word. The foundation of Christianity is *forgiveness* and *mercy*. We follow Jesus Christ who lived and died in forgiveness. His gospel message is restoration, new chances, and the repairing of breaches.

And they that shall be of thee shall build the old waste places: thou shalt raise up the foundations of many generations; and thou shalt be called, The repairer of the breach, The restorer of paths to dwell in. (Isa. 58:12)

Dearly beloved, avenge not yourselves, but rather give place unto wrath: for it is written, Vengeance is mine; I will repay, saith the Lord. (Rom.12:19)

72. HOW MANY TIMES ARE WE EXPECTED TO FORGIVE AN OFFENDER?

Jesus Christ tells us to forgive as many times as an offender asks for forgiveness. We need to forgive even if the offender *has not* asked to be forgiven. Forgiveness is *life*. Jesus knew unforgiveness would *destroy* us.

Jesus taught that it is all right to be angry. Sometimes you *smart* under the injustice of it, and wonder . . . am I a victor or a victim? We have all found we had to forgive and it *has not* always been easy.

Then Peter came to Jesus and asked, 'Lord, how many times shall I forgive my brother when he sins against me? Up to seven times?' Jesus answered, I tell you, not seven times, but seventy-times-seven. (Matt.18:21,22 NIV)

*Dearly beloved, **avenge not yourselves**, but rather give place unto wrath: for it is written, **Vengeance is mine; I will repay**, saith the Lord. (Rom. 12:19)*

73. WHAT IF YOU ARE ONE OF LIFE'S SERIOUS VICTIMS?

We live in a violent society where one out of three women have been sexually abused before 18 years of age. One out of six men have been sexually abused before reaching adulthood. Wife battering happens to 33% of women.

God *sees* it all. He was there (not causing or condoning the abuse) and He hurt when you hurt. He longs for you to come to Him so He can heal your wounds and set you free from the *shame* and the pain.

> *He (Jesus) is despised and rejected of men; a man of sorrows, and acquainted with grief... Surely he hath born our griefs, and carried our sorrows. (Isa. 53: 3,4)*

74. HOW CAN I EVER BE COMPLETELY FREE FROM INNER PAIN?

You begin by admitting you are a *victim*. The pain you feel is really *embarrassment* and *shame*, which is a very typical response. Victims of life's serious offenses feel *defective*. They are sure something is wrong with them or they would never have been victimized.

Recovery from inner pain can be a lifetime work, but with Jesus Christ as your helper and healer, your recovery time can be drastically shortened.

> *The Spirit of the Lord is upon me, because he hath anointed me to preach the gospel to the poor; he hath sent me to* **heal the brokenhearted, to preach deliverance to the captives, and recovering of sight to the blind, to set at liberty them that are bruised.** *(Luke 4: 18)*

75. WHY DID IT HAVE TO HAPPEN TO ME?

Bad things happen to good people. Tragedies happen because tragedies are part of life. Death is part of life. You cannot have life without death, and you cannot have happiness without sadness.

> *Life is not fair, but God is good.*
> *- Robert Schuller*

76. HOW CAN I ESCAPE THIS INNER PRISON?

Freedom and healing occur when you can *acknowledge* and *audibly confess* **it wasn't your fault, you were not to blame, you were a victim of life's tragedies**.

Recovery comes when you can put *full blame* on your abuser and not on yourself. Abused children *can do nothing* to prevent being victimized. **It is not their fault**.

What happened to you is *tragic, but it is not the end.*

You can be healed emotionally and spiritually. God has given you the ability within yourself to write a happy ending. You can accept God's gift to you: **power to forgive yourself**.

> *I the Lord have called thee in righteousness, and will hold thine hand, and will keep thee, and give thee for a covenant of the people, for a light of the Gentiles; to open the blind eyes, **to bring out the prisoners from the prison, and them that sit in darkness out of the prison house**. (Isa. 42:6-7)*

77. WHAT IF I HAVE BEEN THE OFFENDER? CAN I FIND FORGIVENESS?

Yes. For many of us our battle is not with others, it is with ourselves. We are so hesitant to accept God's gift of forgiveness because we feel *we don't deserve it*. We have been the one who did the hurting. We struggle with *shame, remorse and guilt*. How we wish we could undo the things we knew were wrong, cruel and vicious.

You are right, we don't deserve it. But that is exactly why we need it. Forgiveness is God's love in action for people like us who don't deserve it. It is called *grace*!

> *For by grace are ye saved through faith; and that not of yourselves: it is the gift of God: Not of works, lest any man should boast. (Eph. 2: 8,9)*

78. IS FORGIVENESS REALLY IMPORTANT TO US?

It is most important, ***it is life***. We are *lost* without it. We can live with many things but not with guilt and shame. We cannot live without God's forgiveness.

Forgiveness is where we run face-to-face with God's goodness. **If we do not forgive, we cannot be forgiven**.

> *But if ye forgive not men their trespasses, neither will your Father forgive your trespasses.*
> *(Matt. 6:15) Note: See also Matt. 18: 23-35.*

79. HOW DO I RECEIVE IT?

You need to have a personal encounter with the LORD Jesus Christ. Believe on Jesus Christ; believe *He is God.*

You may not be aware of it, but you have been looking for a meeting with Him all of your life. You need to be spiritually born-again. You can't make it without Him.

No one is perfect. We all suffer from guilt and shame. We are all victims. We are all offenders. But Jesus Christ has died on the cross with these final words, *Father, forgive them*! He paid for my crime and yours with His life. The gift of salvation is free... *no strings attached.*

Our great Creator will remove our transgressions, our sins as far as the east is from the west . . . forever! What a comfort! What a relief!

> *And she (the Virgin Mary) shall bring forth a son, and thou shalt call his name JESUS: for he shall save his people from their sins. (Matt. 1:21)*

80.   WHAT WILL HAPPEN WHEN I MEET HIM?

When you find Him, you will find *salvation*. You will learn about the great *forgiver*. You will be saved from shame to glory. He will restore your dignity and self-esteem. Only an act of *divine grace* can accomplish so great a miracle.

*What happens when
life strikes you a blow?
What happens when
you blow it?*

Chapter Seven

Failure Isn't Fatal

Do you not know that you are the temple of God and that the Spirit of God dwells in you? (I Cor. 3:16 NKJ)

*H*ow is your self-image today? Having trouble accepting yourself after goofing, bungling, or sinning? Are you pulled down by a painful awareness of your frailties and your failures?

Whether we want to admit it or not, we all have suffered from the mistakes we have made in life, whether they were intentional or sheer stupidity. Human beings are all prone to make mistakes, *big mistakes*, that can, if we let them, affect the course of our lives. There isn't a single one of us who cannot fall short of our own standards, even stumble, and sin.

What happens when life strikes you a blow? What happens when you "blow it", when you are too weak to resist temptation?

Sin is an act that robs you of your God-given dignity. *Shame* is the first symptom that sin is operating in your life. Nothing blocks the fresh flow of God's Spirit more than a sense of *guilt and shame*. After a defeat, there are down days and moments of discouragement, yet you must resist the temptation to give up on life, that paralyzing emotion or feeling of shame that says, *you cannot go forward*!

You may have collected enough hurts to keep you from wanting to press forward. Setbacks can take the joy out of life if you don't watch out! Be careful! Hidden hurts in the heart can nurture and nourish negative thinking.

Often the most painful wounds are not the scars that are outwardly seen but the hidden wounds deep in the heart. Because they are hidden, they are often the most dangerous. They attach themselves to our souls like parasites, sapping the life and vitality out of us.

Think of the damage that happens in the life of a person who lacks the faith to come home. A shameful act of sin is made worse by the negative reaction it can set off within our lives. The danger is that we'll be too embarrassed to go back again.

Consider:

- the student who flunks out and never returns to the classroom!

- the entrepreneur who suffers a business failure and never starts another business!

- the preacher who fails to practice what he preaches and leaves the ministry.

• the hometown boy who hasn't made good and doesn't dare return to his roots.

Remember that even though you are imperfect, you *still* are a child of God. The power of God within you can *make you* what you ought to be. When once you return to Him in honest confession and genuine repentance, you will discover again the goodness of God, and you will no longer need to run, hide and avoid certain people.

"God likes to *make* people: great people out of common people, strong people out of weak people, famous people out of unknown people, *good people out of bad people*. God makes people not only into what He wants them to be, but also into what they have *always wanted* to become."

To what kind of people does God relate Himself? Imperfect people! There are no other kind. Imperfect people like you and like me. People whom God loves in spite of imperfections and whom God helps to become free of imperfections.

When you stumble, admit you are human. God doesn't expect you to be perfect (yet), but He does expect you to be *dependent on Him*. Failure isn't fatal. You can build again!

Faith is reconstructing after ruin. Faith is learning to walk and learning to bounce back after you stumble and fall. People of faith are *never* ultimately defeated. They simply refuse to take up a permanent residence at a point of failure.

It probably takes more faith to rebuild for a second time than to build the first time. Faith looks at ruin and says, "This only means that you have a chance to build something better in its place."

That's how God is with you and me! Jesus Christ is the Master Craftsman, reconstructing beautiful lives from ruin. A "lost cause" simply doesn't exist in God's mind!

81.   WHAT IS FAILURE?

Failure is a judgment *we make* about unsuccessful events that occur in our life, disappointments that make us feel deficient and/or totally ineffective.

82.   WHY DO WE FAIL?

The basic cause of failure is *fear*. Fear torments your soul and undermines your self-worth. How you feel about yourself determines your level of commitment to a person or thing. A half-hearted commitment will lead to failure.

83.   CAN FEAR OF FAILURE BE A POSITIVE FORCE?

Yes. Fear of failure can keep us going and push us to produce more than we thought we could. The fear of failure can be an insurance policy for success. *Insecurity is the greatest motivator for success.*

84.   HOW DO WE OVERCOME LOW SELF-ESTEEM?

The most effective way to overcome low self-esteem is to turn to prayer. You need to *communicate* with your Creator. He knows what you need. Ask Him! He will tell you.

Chances are you haven't been *listening*; you didn't recognize His voice when He spoke to you. Open your ears and your eyes. You will see God at work in your life.

85. WHAT WILL PRAYER DO FOR ME?

Prayer will give you inner peace and allow you to *look* at your mistakes and *learn* from them. You will also look at your correct answers and *remember* them. Talking to God will turn your attention to *what you have left, not what you have lost.*

86. HOW CAN I STOP BLAMING MYSELF?

You can stop blaming yourself by affirming and believing that the grace of God declares you to be a person made *clean* by the blood of Jesus Christ. God wants you to be a happy, helpful servant, spreading love and encouragement in the world.

We are of little value as long as we carry a negative self-image. Wipe the slate of your soul clean **every night with confession and prayer**. Praise the Lord Jesus Christ for His promised forgiveness and go to sleep knowing there is *no guilt* attached to your record.

87.   CAN GOD USE ME?

God *needs* you. He wants to *use* you. If you ask Him to use you, He will never turn down your generous offer. And when He begins to use you, it is never boring. Life will become one wonderful and exciting event as you discover your life mission.

88.   HOW DO I BEGIN?

Get a new mind set; today is a new day! Set a goal you *know* you can accomplish with the aptitudes you *know* you possess. Be realistic!

Goals have great pulling power. If you set a specific goal, the goal will pull you toward it and you are likely to reach it.

> *Where there is no vision, the people perish...*
> *(Prov. 29:18)*

89.   WHAT IF I DON'T BELIEVE I HAVE A "LIFE MISSION"?

You are not alone. Many of us suffer from low self-esteem that attacks our confidence and cripples us with fear and insecurity. It is not unusual for us to question if we are *worthy* or *talented* enough to be given a life mission.

90.   WILL MY PAST FAILURES MAKE ME INELIGIBLE FOR A MISSION?

Jesus Christ was sent to earth to give man *another chance*. He offers us the opportunity to start again by making us into new creatures. He is the God of multiplied mercies.

He offers a place in His Kingdom to *everyone* who comes to Him to be born-again. He removes the sin, condemnation and guilt from our life and gives us inner joy and peace.

> *There is therefore now no condemnation to them who are in Christ Jesus, who walk not after the flesh, but after the Spirit. (Rom. 8:1)*

91.   IF I HAVE FAILED THE LORD, AM I ELIGIBLE FOR MY MISSION?

If you have *truly* repented, yes! Anyone who ever does anything of consequence for God, must *first* break the shame barrier. Shame was put on Jesus Christ so righteousness could be put on those who failed Him.

The Bible cites examples of men like Abraham, Moses, David, Peter and Paul who failed miserably and were *forgiven* and *restored*.

The call to ministry is given to a man/woman by God

Himself. You cannot call yourself. The gifts and callings of God are *forever*; they are *never retracted*. The Bible contains detailed accounts of the ghastly failings of men chosen by God. However, when they *confessed* their sins and *truly repented*, they found *grace*; they were forgiven and restored.

> *The Jewish High Priest is merely a man like anyone else, but he is chosen to speak for all other men in their dealings with God. He presents their gifts to God and offers to him the blood of animals that are sacrificed to cover the sins of the people and his own sins too. And because he is a man he can deal gently with other men, though they are foolish and ignorant, for he, too, is surrounded with the same temptations and understands their problems very well.*

> *Another thing to remember is that no one can be a high priest just because he wants to be. He has to be called by God for this work in the same way God chose Aaron. (Heb. 5: 1-4 LB)*

> *For the gifts and the calling of God are **irrevocable**. (Rom.11:29 NKJ)*

92. DARE I RISK POSSIBLE FAILURE?

Faith is impossible without risk. Unless you are running the risk of failure, you are *not* totally living within the parameters of faith. God does not promise to bless the *coward*. His promises are packed full of reassurance for those who are *brave* in heart.

Glorious achievements happen when you and I decide to dare to *run the risk* of failure. There is more *self-esteem* generated in honest and noble failure than there is in cowardly retreat from great opportunity.

The Lord is my light and my salvation; whom shall I fear? the Lord is the strength of my life; of whom shall I be afraid?

For in the time of trouble he shall hide me in his pavilion: in the secret of his tabernacle he shall hide me; he shall set me up upon a rock.

And now shall mine head be lifted up above mine enemies round about me: therefore will I offer in his tabernacle sacrifices of joy; I will sing, yea, I will sing praises unto the Lord. (Ps. 27:1,5,6)

You are not a blind victim of heredity with no power to alter your destiny.

Chapter Eight

Your Family Tree

Lo, children are an heritage of the Lord:
and the fruit of the womb is His reward.
(Psalm 127:3)

*T*he most natural and essential way to begin the story of man's life is to give his genealogy; the ancestors and descendants of his *family tree*. The Gospel of Matthew traces the lineage of the persecuted, harassed, wandering Jews from Abraham to the birth of Jesus Christ, the promised Messiah. Through this *family tree* God fulfilled His promise to Abraham, and through his seed all the earth was blessed.

The Bible also records in Genesis the genealogy of Jesus Christ that demonstrates a *faith* rooted in history through this *family tree*. God had promised that the seed of the woman would deal with the serpent and the consequences of his activity among mankind. The careful tracing of the arrival of this *One Promised Seed* is one of Genesis' major themes.

Life lived in the *image of God* is drastically different from life lived in *the likeness of sinful man* as the sad saga of Genesis clearly outlines. It is only as modern man recognizes the difference that he can start coming to grips with life. So long as he sees himself *independent* of God or refuses to *acknowledge* his propensity to sin, modern man is doomed. He repeats the fatal errors of his antediluvian ancestors in more sophisticated and socially acceptable ways. Truly those who refuse to *learn* from history are doomed to repeat it.

The genealogy of Christ, as recorded by Matthew, surprisingly mentions the names of four women: Tamar, Rahab, Ruth and Bathsheba. It was not normal to find in Jewish pedigrees, the names of women, especially women who were all aliens, *Gentiles*. Three of the four women were suspected of adultery. Ruth was a Moabite and the Jewish Law said, *No Ammonite or Moabite may enter the congregation of the Lord. (Deut. 23:3)*

God forgave and accepted in the lineage of Christ, men and women whose history was clouded, to demonstrate ***God does not discriminate against persons because of past mistakes***.

God has a deliberate plan, an advanced plan and design that relates to our *personal salvation*. Who we are by inheritance is *predetermined* by God. He has gone to great pains to mold us into the image He has made us so we can perform His *plan and will*.

93. WHO DECIDED OUR FAMILY HERITAGE?

It was God who determined and transmitted the genes that created your hereditary characteristics and developed the lines of your inheritance which are your *family roots*.

The Scriptures teach our genetic code was decided by our Creator before He laid the foundations of planet Earth.

Your eyes saw my substance, being yet unformed. And in Your book they all were written, The days fashioned for me, When as yet there were none of them. (Ps. 139:16 NKJ)

94. WHO AND WHAT DETERMINED OUR PHYSICAL CHARACTERISTICS AND APPEARANCE?

God used what scientists now call DNA *in the process*. When a child is conceived, half of his DNA inheritance comes from the father and half from the mother. In the microscopic fertilized egg, the joined DNA forms a six foot long, helix-shaped genetic ladder that is compacted within a tiny egg.

Every detail of our physical being is programmed by DNA. Its intricacies far outweigh the most sophisticated computer system available today. The color of your hair was pre-programmed by your DNA. The shape of your nose, your height, your body frame, all your physical characteristics were determined at the moment of conception.

95. WHAT MAKES ME DIFFERENT?

Your natural gifts make you different. Just as DNA eventually brings forth our physical characteristics, so God built into us *gifts* to shape our personality and to become the motivating force for our lives. Your own *giftedness* is a priceless possession, something already *given* to each of us by God at our creation.

> *So, we, being many, are one body in Christ, and **individually** members of one another. Having then gifts **differing** according to the grace that is given to us, let us use them: (Rom. 12:5,6 NKJ)*

96. HOW DO NATURAL GIFTS SHAPE OUR PERSONALITY?

Our *gifts* are the motivating force of our lives, and determine the course we will pursue throughout our lifetime. Our *motivational gifts* bring forth the interests, abilities, enthusiasms, and actions that make us effective.

97. WHAT INFLUENCES US MOST IN THE WAY WE GROW?

Your birth order. It has a powerful influence on the

YOUR FAMILY TREE

kind of person you will be. Everyone develops a style
of life while growing up. Our style of life is our per-
ception of *how* we fit into our world.

Your birth order was planned by God. He knew the
time and place of your birth. He planned it all.

> *To everything on earth there is a season... a time to
> be born ... (Eccl. 3:1,2)*

98. PLEASE DEFINE "BIRTH ORDER."

There are three main birth order positions, and *each*
order has its definite personality distinction:

1. The oldest child, or the only child.
2. The second, or middle-born children.
3. The youngest - the family baby, last born.

99. WHAT ARE THE CHARACTERISTICS OF THE OLDEST OR ONLY CHILD?

The oldest or only child becomes the *Guinea Pig* for
brand-new parents. He or she is the main attraction
and everything they do is a **big deal**. They are usually over-protected and over-disciplined. Because they
usually have only adult models to imitate, they mimic
adult ways and this often presents problems in relating
to their peers.

The oldest or only children soon become aware of the

special *first-born* status and perceive they are expected to be responsible and very disciplined, so they strive to please because of the pressures imposed upon them to be the *perfect children*. Early in life, they develop into authorative persons who will strive to preserve the family pride, values and traditions.

100. WHAT ARE THE CHARACTERISTICS OF THE SECOND OR MIDDLE CHILD?

When the second-born child enters the family, he usually becomes the *opposite* of the first born. He chooses his lifestyle by what he perceives, so he might become a manipulator or a controller, a victim or a martyr, a pleaser or an antagonizer. The middle child will always feel *squeezed* from above and below.

The middle child is very *competitive* and early in life develops social skills and a *free spirit*. He will usually be the first one to venture out of the family circle to seek a group he sees as *his*, that will afford him the same privileges he perceives as belonging to the oldest child.

101. WHAT ARE THE CHARACTERISTICS OF THE YOUNGEST, THE FAMILY BABY, THE LAST BORN?

By the time the last child is born, the parents are usually tired and have a tendency to let the last born get by with many things they forbid their older children.

There is also the tendency to let the last born shift for himself or get most of his instructions from his brothers and sisters.

Last born can take a lot of abuse, pressure, resentment and teasing from older siblings. They get used to being *put down* by their siblings and grow up with an, *I'll show them!* attitude.

Because they are not taken seriously, they have a compelling desire to make an important contribution to the world. They can be very positive, competitive and become outstanding athletes. The youngest is typically outgoing, charming, personable, affectionate and uncomplicated, but a *great manipulator*. It is not unusual for them to show off, playing the "clown" to get attention, be irresponsible and expect someone else to do things for them.

102. WHICH BIRTH ORDER IS MORE DESIRABLE?

No birth order is better. Every birth order has inherent strengths and weaknesses. First-born seem to have a corner on achievement, but the door is wide open for later born to make their mark. It is up to them.

Birth order is **only** an influence. The way parents treat their children is equally important to birth order.

103. WHAT PURPOSE DID GOD HAVE IN PREORDAINING OUR HERITAGE?

Our giftedness was not an after-thought. God programmed our gifts, aptitudes and personality into our *members* to enable us to accomplish our mission on earth. It was all part of God's plan to shape us for our role in the building of His Kingdom.

> *And we know that **all things** work together for good to those who love God, to those who **are the called according to His purpose**. For whom He foreknew, He also predestined to be conformed to the image of His Son, that He might be the firstborn among many brethren. (Rom. 8:28-29 NKJ)*

104. HOW DOES A DYSFUNCTIONAL, TROUBLED FAMILY FIT INTO HIS PLAN?

It was never God's intent to bring children into a dysfunctional, troubled family. The neurotic family life is damaging to a child's budding self-image and self-esteem and results in spiritual retardation.

For many persons the natural taproot of *faith* is severed or poisoned by physical, sexual, emotional, verbal or spiritual abuse. But it need not be *fatal*, that is, if *reality* is faced.

105. IS IT POSSIBLE TO OVERCOME THE DAMAGE A DYSFUNCTIONAL, TROUBLED FAMILY INFLICTS?

Yes, it is possible **if** you come to terms with reality and accept and admit your heritage was *despicable. Face your fears!* Don't run from them. If you can face them, you can erase their damaging effects on your self-image. Our earliest environment often gives us a picture of ourselves as weak, mentally below-average, and destined to experience certain *failure.*

To some degree the earlier feeling *will always be there*, but we can act in harmony with God and an entirely new self-image will emerge. **If** you forget the *if only* syndrome, *(If only I had been born into another family! If only I had another mother or father!)* and begin to say: *at least, nevertheless, however, the next time*, you can experience a true change.

106. WHAT IF YOU FEEL SHAME ABOUT YOUR ROOTS?

Your parents may have been rebels against great family values and traditions that brought pain and shame. God has a remedy for this: He puts a shining *solitaire* in **every** family.

If you look for them, you can and you will find someone in your past who had *noble values.* Don't be afraid to check out the family tree. You may find a problem or a skeleton in your closet, but you'll undoubtedly find some honorable and inspiring souls, too.

God sets the solitary in families. (Ps. 68:6 NKJ)

107. HOW CAN I BE PROUD OF MY FAMILY?

What is there about your family that makes you feel *ashamed*? Is it their language skills, physical features, skin color, culture, their ethnic style of dress? Look again; you may discover something wonderful to make you very proud of your family.

A few years ago Alex Haley wrote a heart-wrenching history of the Americans of African ancestry. *Roots* was made into a dramatic screen play for television. The television program captured the attention of millions of viewers, and troubled the nation's conscience.

Roots produced two entirely different reactions in the black community. It incited anger, a violent anger for revenge, and gave many disgruntled people a *reason* for poverty, failure and low-self esteem.

But *Roots* also produced another effect. The history of the black people lifted their self-esteem. It instilled a great sense of *pride* in being African-Americans because now they realized they had such a *tough* and *strong lineage*. Their ancestors **were able to endure** the brutal humiliation of being kidnaped and sold by

104

their own people, inhuman passage across dangerous seas, persecution, epidemic, plagues and *generations of cruel slavery* because they were **survivors**. They survived for a *purpose* - God's purpose - to bring **today's African Americans** into existence.

108. HOW CAN I RESTORE DIGNITY TO MY FAMILY TREE?

If you are determined to *upgrade* your family name, start by doing a better job of parenting than your father and mother. *Learn* from their mistakes. *Correct the errors* in instruction you picked up from them. *Redeem* the honor of your family name by becoming the kind of a person that will *restore dignity and respect* to your family tree.

We are *not* blind victims of heredity or environment, with *no power* to alter our destiny. There is a *divine inner-capacity* which enables us to be *more* than we are. It is important we *do not deceive ourselves*. Recognize the *deep inner feelings* planted there long ago by your Creator which still reside within. **There is a divine destiny to your life. Discover it!**

> *For you did not receive the spirit of bondage again to fear, but you received the Spirit of adoption by whom we cry out, "Abba, Father." The Spirit Himself bears witness with our spirit that we are children of God. (Rom. 8: 15,16 NKJ)*

109. WHAT IF I HAVE NO FAMILY?

Then you need to find a *family* and become a *part* of it. That's what the Church offers. You can become a part of the *Family of God*. **And what a family it is!**

By His death and resurrection, Jesus Christ made it possible for everyone who believes in Him to be brought into a special relationship with God, *an adoption into His family*. The Holy Spirit releases in us the *spirit of adoption*, a deep and miraculous assurance of love, acceptance and belonging, thus filling the void. Thank God, there is Someone who can fill this void and give you the identity and love you crave: Jesus Christ.

You can sing this song; sing it with true conviction and great assurance:

> *"I'm so glad I belong*
> *to the family of God,*
> *I've been washed in His fountain,*
> *Cleansed by His blood.*
>
> *Joint heirs with Jesus,*
> *As I travel this sod;*
> *For I'm a part of His family,*
> *The family of God."*

> *Bill Gathier 1974*

Promotion depends on faithfulness in natural things.

CHAPTER NINE

Make Me A Servant

I will arise and go to my father, and will say unto him,
Father, I have sinned against heaven, and before thee, and
am no more worthy to be called thy son: make me as one
of thy hired servants. (Luke 15:18,19)

S everal years ago, my mother, Pastor M. D. Beall, preached a sermon at Bethesda Missionary Temple in Detroit, Michigan, about the ***Prodigal Son***. She developed her sermon around a *very different interpretation* of the familiar story Jesus told His disciples. The message surprised and stirred the Sunday morning audience. In fact, it struck a spiritual nerve, much like a dentist who, looking for cavities in his patient's teeth, happens upon an exposed nerve.

This Prodigal Son *was not* the traditional willful, rebel-lious, younger son written about in the Gospel of Luke, but rather, he was a *Believer* who came to his Father and asked Him for *all* that he had coming to him by inheritance.

The Father without hesitation gave his son his inheritance. He filled him with the precious gift of His Spirit. He called him into a particular branch of His service. He made him aware there were *specific* spiritual gifts he should earnestly covet. These were the *special* gifts the Father had written in his members before he was born, to enable him to successfully accomplish his mission; they would develop over time with exercise.

The son eagerly took all of his priceless inheritance the Father bestowed upon him. The Father was pleased and looked forward to helping him develop character skills to enhance his inheritance.

The Father appointed tutors and governors to train his son in investing and multiplying his inheritance. But instead of giving himself to prayer and studying God's Word, to learn how to protect and invest his inheritance and increase it, he grew restless. The Father's admonitions to teach him how he could best accomplish his mission, by learning how to master the art, instruction and discipline of discipleship, were ignored. It grieved the Father to see him resist his will.

The son wanted action. The discipline of the Father's house was too strict. He wanted something more. *And not many days after, the younger son gathered all together and took his journey into a far country.* He packed his bags and impulsively left home and his Father to make a name for himself in the religious world.

In search of a spiritual high, instant success, excitement, popularity and fame, he traveled from one revival meeting to another. He plunged himself into any and every new religious movement; he was seeking "truth". The men and women he met along the way were just like him: enthusiasts, unstable, thrill-seekers who were looking for the *new thing*.

His new friends took advantage of his inheritance, the *fresh* anointing upon his life, and drained it from him as they traveled with him. Religious opportunists saw his potential and encouraged him to exploit his gifts of faith and power for popularity and fame. But *with no time* to pray and fellowship with Jesus Christ, he soon lost power.

So he succumbed to *short cuts* and began to think up silly ideas of what God was like and what He wanted them to do... making merchandise of the Gospel with questionable doctrines and practices to maintain momentum.

It was a sad day, the day he finally admitted *he had nothing left; he had squandered his inheritance*. The false prophets and "spiritual, moral harlots", who merge with anyone or anything for their own advantage, had spent or taken away everything he possessed. He was totally bankrupt!

And he began to be in want. The anointing he had taken for granted was gone. The peace and joy of the Lord were nowhere to be found. His precious inheritance had been squandered. He had ended up living and feeding with the pigs: the evil, the unclean, the reprobate. He smelt like them, he looked like them... he was now *one of them*.

He was so spiritually hungry, he would have eaten anything - even the food the pigs were eating, but they refused to give him anything to satisfy his deep soul yearnings. In this darkest night of his soul, sorrow and remorse racked his body and mind day after day.

But that is not the end of the story. Back at the ranch his Father was continually praying and watching for him. He never gave up on his son. And the day came when the godly sorrow that racked his son's body and soul *worked repentance... and he came to himself!*

For the first time in his life he realized the wonderful life of security and peace the *servants* of his Father enjoyed. Why, they had plenty to eat *and to spare!* And here he was perishing with hunger, wallowing in filth, eating with the swine, living in poverty and despair. And in that moment of enlightenment, *faith* arose in his soul... **he knew he could go home!**

I am going home! I am going home! He shouted and cried, tears flooded his dirty face and ran down his pungent, putrid garments. *I will say to my Father, I have sinned against heaven and in thy sight. I am no more worthy to be called your son...* **Father, make me as one of your hired servants!**

The Father knew his son would return home someday, when he realized the value of home and the blessings of servanthood. He was patiently waiting for his return. The Father saw him coming when he was still a great distance from home, and he ran to meet him. Weeping for joy, the father embraced him. The son fell at his Father's feet in repentance and begged, **"Father, make me!"**

And what did the Father do? He called the servants to bring him the *best* robe, and shoes for his feet, and a ring for his son's finger. He ordered the fatted calf to be killed and a meal prepared for a *big* celebration. *This my son was dead, but he is alive again!*

110. WHAT DOES IT MEAN TO BE A SERVANT?

A servant is one who serves his Master with love and devotion. He has a desire to extend to others the same love and service which the Father extends to him through His Son.

How true it is that a servant is not greater than his master. Nor is the messenger more important than the one who sends him. You know these things - now do them! That is the path of blessing. (John 13:16-17 LB)

111. WHERE AND HOW DO WE BEGIN?

There is a natural process to go through, in which God trains you for reigning. If you try to convert the world without this understanding, you are doomed to failure. There is a great journey between being *born again* and *reigning* with Christ. We are not born again and given great spiritual responsibility immediately. We must grow to a level of understanding and capability before we are allowed to *solo*.

Newborn Christians need instruction and discipline. We call this **discipleship**.

Now I say, that the heir, as long as he is a child, dif-

fereth nothing from a servant, though he be lord of all, but is under tutors and governors until the time appointed of the father. (Gal. 4: 1,2)

Take my yoke upon you, and learn of me; for I am meek and lowly in heart: and ye shall find rest unto your souls. (Matt. 11:29)

112. PLEASE DEFINE DISCIPLESHIP.

Christian discipleship is related to the goal of encouraging and measuring growth in *behavioral change*. It results from a consistent application of biblical principles to personal and corporate Christian living.

God will use and promote the believer who drinks the milk of the Word faithfully each day and uses the strength and wisdom derived from it to obey the Holy Spirit in the small, everyday things. When believers begin to chew on tender meat, and then the tougher meat of the Word, they begin to conquer challenges in their life and bear some fruit. One of the greatest challenges is *learning to control the flesh and become like Jesus in godly character*.

113. WHAT IS CONSIDERED CHRIST-LIKE BEHAVIOR?

Christ-like behavior includes: integrity, honor, faithfulness, loyalty, perseverance and honesty. This means paying your bills, training and instructing your children, disciplining yourself to attend church services, prayer meeting and choir practice on time. It includes good works, like helping a family with food or care when there is a desperate need.

God was pleased with Jesus because He had been faithful to study and pray, establishing a strong relationship with the Father. He also honored His earthly father and mother. He respected the Jewish traditions and developed godly character. Jesus could be counted on.

For if any be a hearer of the word, and not a doer, he is like unto a man beholding his natural face in a glass: For he beholdeth himself, and goeth his way, and straightway forgetteth what manner of man he was. But whoso looketh into the perfect law of liberty, and continueth therein, he being not a forgetful hearer, but a doer of the work, this man shall be blessed in his deed. (Jas. 1: 23-25)

114. HOW DO YOU LEARN TO RULE YOUR OWN SPIRIT?

To overcome the temptations of the flesh, a believer must *learn* to *rule* his mind, his emotions and his will *by his own spirit*. Change comes from the inside out. The biggest battles of life are in the realm of our soul. You will be strengthened and directed by the Holy Spirit if you stay focused on the Word of God. God's Word brings peace in the midst of life's storms.

But I keep under my body, and bring it into subjec-
tion: lest that by any means, when I have preached
to others, I myself should be a castaway.
(I Cor. 9: 27)

115. HOW IMPORTANT IS ORDER IN OUR FAMILY?

The Apostle Paul told the Elders they **could not** rule
the house of God unless they demonstrated they could
rule their own households well, ruling their families *in*
love and training their children in the discipline and
instruction of the Lord.

Ruling your own house applies to the single person as
well as the married. The *single person* is responsible
to develop an excellent lifestyle that enhances his reputation in moral behavior, his work habits, honest
dealings with finances, his appearance, his dwelling
place and his possessions.

As far back as I can remember, my brothers and I were
strongly admonished *to be an example to the flock.*
That meant our appearance, manners, behavior,
housekeeping, finances and lifestyle. You cannot pastor a church or be a leader in any dimension when
your own home is in chaos.

Men and women should not lead a Bible study if they
can't keep a clean house and a tidy yard, and instruct
their own children in the Word. God isn't going to

give positions of authority to people who have never learned to tend their own personal business.

116. IS IT TRUE THAT FAITHFULNESS IN NATURAL THINGS BRINGS REVELATION IN SPIRITUAL THINGS?

Yes. Cleaning your house, washing the car, ironing your clothes, bathing and putting on deodorant, paying the bills - those are *natural things* and they are important. They are important because the outward life is what constitutes a believer's witness to the world that Jesus Christ can save, heal, deliver, and make the difference in a person's life.

It is wrong to say *natural things* don't matter because we are going to do spiritual work. The truth is, in many cases the spiritual work will not happen *until* we are producing fruit in the natural areas of our lives.

There is a natural body and there is a spiritual body. God teaches His children spiritual reality and principles through the knowledge and application of natural principles. The natural is *first*. The spiritual is *second*. If you're not faithful cutting the grass and parking cars, you aren't going to be faithful ruling in the Church. If you won't obey your parents, you won't obey the Holy Spirit. If you won't follow instructions on a test in school or a project at work, you won't line up with the Word of God.

117. WHY ARE NATURAL THINGS SO IMPORTANT?

God says to let a man be *proven* at home before you lay hands on him and give him a place of authority in the church.

> *For if a man know not how to rule his own house, how shall he take care of the church of God?* (I Tim. 3:5)

Too many people get *religious* and then quit paying their bills, washing their cars, and supporting their families. They totally disregard everything else that speaks of character. You visit them in their homes and it looks like a wreck!

Many people set their goals to be an elder, a worship leader, a Bible teacher, or some position in the church, and they conveniently forget about their *responsibilities* to their families and employers. Faithfulness in the natural means you are *obedient* to do the mundane, everyday things without any thought of whether or not it will bring you a spiritual reward.

Excitement and enthusiasm should not distract believers from being obedient and responsible. This is maturity! Faithfulness in the natural things reflects the heart of God. The greatest *ability* you'll ever have is *dependability*. You can be counted on.

118. DOES FAITHFULNESS INVOLVE MONEY?

Yes. Responsible, dependable saints pay their bills. They work for their income. They are not religious leeches. They support the Kingdom of God with their tithes, they support missions, they give offerings to the Lord and alms to the poor. They have learned *through experience that* **God is their source of supply**.

Give, and it shall be given unto you; good measure, pressed down, and shaken together, and running over, shall men give into your bosom. For with the same measure that ye mete withal it shall be measured to you again. (Luke 6:38)

119. WHERE DOES GREATNESS BEGIN?

Jesus taught His disciples, "If you would be great in my Kingdom, you must *learn* to be **servant of all**. Whoever desires to be great among you let him be your *servant*. And whoever desires to become great among you, let him be your slave..." (Matt 20:26-27) If you don't like to do natural things, you won't like serving God. You won't be promoted if you're not willing to get your hands dirty. Promotion depends on faithfulness in natural things.

A true disciple does not witness and pray on his *employer's time*. A lot of people get fired because they are lazy or act stupid, not because they are spiritual. If you neglect your responsibilities in natural things you are no more spiritual than the heathen.

120. WHAT ARE THE REWARDS OF FAITHFULNESS?

• Faithfulness rewards us with many opportunities.

• Faithfulness rewards us with victory over difficulties.

• Faithfulness is rewarded with increase.

> *... for God resisteth the proud, and giveth grace to the humble. Humble yourselves therefore under the mighty hand of God, that he may exalt you in due time. (I Peter 5: 5,6)*

121. IS THERE AN APPOINTED TIME FOR PROMOTION?

Yes! The Father's method of preparing and maturing disciples involves placing them under tutors and governors *until the time appointed of the Father*. **That is how Jesus started. This is where all faithful men and women, who are destined to rule and reign with Christ, have their start.** Being faithful in the natural, everyday, mundane things of life, is the beginning of becoming great in the Kingdom of God.

> *If you would be great in My Kingdom,*
> *Learn to be servant of all.*
> *I'll open a river when you are a giver,*
> *And learn to be servant of all. (Unknown)*

*Lord, give me patience...
but I want it now!*

Chapter Ten

Faith And Patience

Do not let this happy trust in the Lord die away, no matter what happens... You need to keep on patiently doing God's will if you want him to do for you all that he has promised.
(Heb. 10:35-36 LB)

I have discovered, both through biblical study and personal experience, that the way God thinks of *time* is very different from our way of thinking. He never seems to be in a hurry, yet He is always right on time, and He takes considerably more time than we like to wait, before He brings His promises to pass.

Some of the greatest failures of the heroes of the Bible resulted from their impatience to *wait* for God's promises to be fulfilled. Abraham thought he was running out of time and he and Sarah tried to *help* God bring His promise of a child to pass with the birth of *Ishmael*.

King Saul thought Samuel was taking too long to come and officiate the offering to the Lord. So he "forced himself" to start the service without Samuel. His impatience and disobedience cost Saul and his descendants, the right to reign on the throne of the Kingdom of Israel. Whenever we run ahead of God and try to fulfill His promises, we will live to regret what we have done.

When Jesus heard His friend Lazarus was critically ill, He purposely waited four more days before He went to him. The disciples thought Jesus went too late and His delay offended Mary and Martha; they told Him so!

When Jesus and the disciples arrived, Lazarus was in the tomb and his flesh was already decaying. That was exactly what Jesus wanted to happen. He wanted them to know He is **Resurrection and Life!** His timing was perfect. He miraculously raised Lazarus from the dead, and God received the glory!

The Master has the *final decision* about the time of fulfilling His promises. Jesus continues to demonstrate His power over situations. It may look like it is too late for any help: the marriage may be in the divorce court, the business may be heading for bankruptcy, the ministry opportunities may be gone, the doctors may have given up hope, age and health may be against you, a storm may be heading for your home... BUT GOD will come through *on time* - His time! When we learn God has His own time schedule we can enter into His *rest* and wait on Him.

> *For ye have need of patience, that, **after** ye have done the will of God, ye might receive the promise. For yet a little while, and he that shall come will*

come, and will not tarry. (Heb. 10: 36-37)

Have you ever smarted with frustration when a sincere friend told you, "Don't worry, dear; it will happen in God's time!"? We often resent and reject that comment because we think we know better. We are certain our faith can force God to work on our time schedule. Why? Because, we reason, we know how desperately we want and need it *now*. Tomorrow would simply be too late.

Waiting on God's time schedule can be a frustration to the flesh, a trying of the *patience* of the saints. Come on now, admit it. Who hasn't tried to use our "faith" to force God to act on our time schedule? We have all prayed for "patience" but we want it NOW!

122. WHAT IS THE PURPOSE OF GOD GIVING MAN HIS PROMISES?

God knows His promises to His people are necessary in the building of an intimate relationship with Him. How else would we know and trust Him? When we believe God's promise to us it banishes **fear**, it promotes **faith** and it makes us aware of **the future**.

123. HOW DOES GOD'S PROMISE BANISH FEAR?

David repeatedly praised God's Word in his Psalms, for he learned the entrance of God's Word into his heart gave him peace and banished fear. He learned over time that he could trust God. God cannot lie!

The entrance of thy words giveth light; it giveth

understanding unto the simple. (Psa. 119:130)

124. HOW DO GOD'S PROMISES PRODUCE FAITH?

God stimulates *faith* through His word so we can learn to trust the Lord for all that we are unable to do for ourselves. God proclaims His truth through His word in order that men and women might believe Him and trust Him to be *all* that they could ever wish for in time and eternity.

> *Abraham believed in the Lord, and He counted it to him for righteousness. (Gen. 15:6)*

125. DO GOD'S PROMISES UNVEIL THE FUTURE?

Yes. Only God knows the future, but He does! When He gives a promise to us of things to come, He knows exactly how it will come to pass, how long it will take and the events that must occur before the promise is fulfilled. When we believe His promises, we have a goal to reach for, a *hope* for the future.

The Lord promised Abraham that he would possess the land of Israel and even gave him geographic details of its borders. There are some well-known members of Israel's Parliament who look at this promise *today* for a rationale for their policies of annexation and development by settlement, in what others call the Occupied Territories. The promises of God continue to stimulate faith, calm fears and give *hope* for the future.

> *For all the promises of God in him (Christ), are yea and in him Amen, unto the glory of God by us. (2 Cor. 1:20)*

126. WHY IS PATIENCE NECESSARY TO INHERIT GOD'S PROMISES?

Even though we enjoy a special relationship with God, we are not exempt from the circumstances of life and the reactions common to man. Neither do we enter into the place of blessing without pain and trial. There are some of the promises that can only be fulfilled through much horror and not a little darkness. **You can only inherit the promises of God with faith and patience;** there are no shortcuts. Tribulation works *patience*.

There is also the *perfect* timing of God. When God told Abraham there would be a delay of "four hundred years" or to "the fourth generation", before his descendants would inherit the Promised Land, he, no doubt had many questions and wondered about such things. But God knew Abram could not possibly subdue the land with his own limited resources. But there was a much more profound reason for the delay.

The Lord explained, *In the fourth generation they*

shall return here, for the iniquity of the Amorites is not yet complete. In other words, God knew the people of Canaan could not be judged by Him through His people without there being proper reason for such judgment. He was not arbitrarily deciding to kick the Amorites out so that His favorites could take their place. His people were going to be the means to achieving His divine ends, but His divine ends were going to be impeccably just. Moreover, the Lord who knows the end from the beginning knew exactly how long it would take these people to become totally corrupt. A sobering reminder of the sovereign knowledge and will of God!

> *And therefore will the Lord wait, that he may be gracious unto you, and therefore will he be exalted, that he may have mercy upon you: for the Lord is a God of judgment: blessed are all they that wait for him. (Isa. 30:18)*

127. DOES TRIBULATION REALLY WORK PATIENCE IN US?

Most certainly! I received a promise through prophecy that the books I would write would be sent around the world and taught internationally. It took forty years of highs and lows, questions and doubts as well as seasons of high hopes and faith. That's the way our relationship with our Master is developed and matured. I learned by experience God has a *time* and a *season* for His promises to be fulfilled.

Why did it take so long to bring this particular promise to pass? The Russian translation of *Understanding God and His Covenants*, would not have been accepted in the Soviet Union until the Communists were no longer in power. God knew that! He waited until the Communist Party fell and then he made the Russian translation a reality. Amazing, isn't it?

128. DO THE SCRIPTURES MAKE REFERENCE TO GOD'S TIMING?

Yes. Here are some scripture references:

*When the **fullness of time** had come, God sent forth His Son. (Gal. 4:4 NKJ)*

*Jesus Christ gave Himself a ransom for all, to be testified in **due time**. (I Tim.2:6)*

*In **due time** Christ died for the ungodly. (Rom. 5:6)*

*In the dispensation of the **fullness of time**, God might gather together in one all things in Christ. (Eph. 1:10)*

*To everything there is a **season**, and a **time** to every purpose under heaven... a **time** for every work... everything beautiful **in His time**. (Ecc. 3:1,11,17)*

*It is not for you to know the **times or the seasons**,*

*which the Father has put in His own power. But you shall receive power **after that** the Holy Ghost is come. (Acts 1:7-8)*

*Until the **time** that his (Joseph's) word (of prophecy) came, the word of the Lord tested him. (Psa. 105:19)*

*And let us not grow weary while doing good, for in **due season** we shall reap if we do not lose heart. (Gal. 6:9 NKJ)*

129. WHAT DOES GOD MEAN WHEN HE SAYS, "SUDDENLY" OR "IMMEDIATELY"?

When God uses the word *suddenly* or *immediately*, it may seem a sudden event has happened spontaneously. However, if we look below the surface, we find a long time of preparation has led up to the sudden manifestation.

The coming of the Holy Spirit was not an unexpected surprise from God, which no one had prepared for or expected to receive. One hundred and twenty followers of Jesus had been together in the upper room awaiting its arrival.

And suddenly there came a sound from heaven as of a rushing mighty wind, and it filled all the house where they were sitting. (Acts 2:2)

The word *immediately* was used by Jesus in a similar way. He compared the establishment of His Kingdom to the planting of seed. He spoke of the *immediate harvest* at the end of the age. Yet, the harvest only comes after the seed has been planted, germinated, sprouted and produced a mature stalk of grain. When the grain is fully ripe *then immediately* the farmer comes and harvests it. *Sudden and Immediate* are based on progressive growth and preparation. We have all heard of "over-night-success" stories, that took 20 years to happen.

130. HOW DOES THIS COMPARE WITH GOD'S PROMISES TO US?

A vision, a ministry or project are planted in our spirit as a *seed.* Over time it grows without notice to ourselves or others, but we keep praying, waiting and believing. But *suddenly*, when it has reached full maturity, when the person, the ministry, God's purposes are ready, then *immediately* God harvests it by bringing it into full activity and fulfillment, and manifests it to the Church and the world.

131. WHAT IS MEANT BY "NOW" OR "THIS DAY"?

We interpret *now* and *this day* to mean within twenty-four hours. Not so in God's time table.

When King Saul failed to obey a command from the

Lord through the Prophet Samuel, the Prophet told him **now** *his kingdom would be taken from him*. It did not come to pass until **thirty-eight** years later.

A few years later, Samuel gave Saul another prophecy that he did not obey. Samuel spoke another word of judgment: *The Lord has torn the kingdom of Israel from you **this day**, and he has given it to a neighbor of yours that is better than you. (I Sam 28:17)*

It was about **twenty-four years** later that the kingdom was transferred to David.

132. IS THERE A GUIDE TO HELP US FIGURE GOD'S TIME TABLE?

Yes, I came across such a time table in Bill Hamon's book, *"Prophets and Personal Prophecy"*. I have found the following timetable for prophetic terminology helpful, but not rigid:

- **Immediately** means from one day to three years.

- **Very soon** means one to ten years.

- **I will** without a definite time designation, means God will act sometime in the person's life, **if** he is obedient.

- **Soon** was the term Jesus Christ used to describe the time of His soon return, almost two thousand years ago. *Behold, I come quickly!*

*You have a calling
which exists for
"only you".*

*"Only you" can
fulfill it.*

CHAPTER ELEVEN

Discovering Your Gifts

... that you may prove what is that good, and acceptable,
and perfect will of God concerning you.
(Rom. 12: 2)

As a young woman, I spent many sleepless, fretful nights in the woman's dormitory of the Bible College I attended in Springfield, Missouri, praying and inquiring of the Lord why I was there, and wondering if I would ever know God's plan and purpose for my life. My fears were not unique. My classmates had their share of similar misgivings. Here we were, far from home, endeavoring to prepare ourselves for some type of Christian service and the majority of us did not have the faintest or foggiest idea *how or where* we would fit.

Our prayers did not go unnoticed by our heavenly Father. In His perfect timing, the Lord sent another mighty spiritual renewal to His Church to restore and activate the *gifts* He had won for them. The wind of the Spirit began to blow upon the Church. What had happened on the day of Pentecost happened again. Life was restored *as sons and daughters, men and women began to prophesy.* The prophetic word created new life as spiritual gifts of *utterance, power and revelation* were restored to the Church.

The Lord Jesus Christ **descended** into the lower parts of the earth, after His death by crucifixion, to defeat Satan and strip him of his power. He took the keys of death, hell and the grave and **ascended** victoriously with a multitude of the saints of ages past, and *the spoils of the battle* in His hands.

He gave *five Ministry Gifts* - *Apostles, Prophets, Evangelists, Pastors and Teachers* to appointed men and women, to equip His Church and enable them to continue His ministry on earth as His true representatives.

> *And His gifts were (varied; He Himself appointed and gave men to us,) some to be **apostles** (special messengers), some **prophets**, (inspired preachers and expounders), some **evangelists** (preachers of the Gospel, traveling missionaries), some **pastors** (shepherds of His flock) and **teachers**.* (Eph. 4:11 AMP)

The gifts of Christ fall into *three* unique categories: the five *Ministry* Gifts, **Manifested** *Gifts, and what has recently been termed "in thee gifts" or* **Motivational** *Gifts.*

There are **nine Manifested Gifts**, supernatural manifestations of the Holy Spirit that work *through* a believer. They are: wisdom, knowledge, faith, healings, miracles, prophecy, discerning of spirits, various kinds of tongues and the interpretation of tongues.

But to each one is given the manifestation of the Spirit - that is, the evidence, the spiritual illumination of the Spirit - for good and profit. To one is given in and through the (Holy) Spirit (the power to speak) a message of wisdom, and to another (the power to express) a word of knowledge and understanding according to the same (Holy) Spirit. To another (wonder working) faith by the same (Holy) Spirit, to another the extraordinary powers of healing by the one Spirit;

To another the working of miracles, to another prophetic insight - that is, the gift of interpreting the divine will and purpose; to another the ability to discern and distinguish between (the utterance of true) spirits (and false ones), to another various kinds of (unknown) tongues, to another the ability to interpret (such) tongues. (I Cor. 12: 7-10)

Motivational Gifts hold the key to understanding many things about yourself: why you think and act the way you do, how you relate to other people and circumstances around you, and what makes you the special individual you are. There are **seven motivational gifts** mentioned in the Bible: prophet or perceiver, server, teacher, exhorter, giver, administrator and a comforter, encourager.

As each of you has received a gift (a particular spiritual talent, a gracious divine endowment), employ it for one another as (befits) good trustees of God's many-sided grace - faithful stewards of the extremely divers (powers and gifts granted to Christians by) unmerited favor. (I Peter 4: 10 TAB)

CONCERNING SPIRITUAL GIFTS

Paul the Apostle exhorted Timothy not to neglect the gifts that were in him, but to keep them *active* and *alive*. We humans need constant prodding or we soon fall back to our old habits. Spiritual gifts become carnal when they are not activated by the Holy Spirit, for they lose their power and can only produce dead works.

> *Neglect not the gift that is in you, which was given to you by prophecy with the laying on of the hands of the eldership. (I Tim. 4:14 NKJ)*

A careful examination of this verse, as given in *The Interlinear Greek-English New Testament*, brings out an interesting rendering: "Be not negligent of the **in thee gift** which was given thee through prophecy with the laying on of the hands of the Presbytery."

The original Greek refers to the ***in thee gift***, indicating that the *gift* was already "in" Timothy when the elders prayed for him. The word "given" in the Greek is *didomi* which has a wide range of meanings according to *Strong's Exhaustive Concordance of the Bible* including "to be brought forth, shown, and uttered."

Timothy had not identified his natural giftings. He was unaware of the *purpose* God had for his life. When the gift of Prophecy and the Word of Knowledge *verbally identified his gifting* by the Presbytery, it was **uncovered** and **activated; life was breathed into it** by the Holy Spirit.

The seven motivational gifts, mentioned in Scripture, are the special abilities and gifts God *wrote* into our members, gifts that are *born* in us. They are indeed what the original

Greek refers to as the "in thee gift," indicating that the gift was already in believers when the Presbytery prayed for them, waiting to be uncovered.

> *Having gifts (faculties, talents, qualities) that differ according to the grace given us, let us use them: (He whose gift is)* **prophecy***, (let him prophesy) according to the proportion of his faith; (He whose gift is)* **practical service***, let him give himself to serving; he who* **teaches***, to his teaching; (He who* **exhort, encourages***), to his exhortation; he who* **contributes***, let him do it in simplicity and liberality; he who* **gives aid and superintends***, with zeal and singleness of mind; he who does* **acts of mercy***, with genuine cheerfulness and joyful eagerness.*
> *(Rom. 12: 6-8 TAB)*

Our prior lessons have made us aware our Creator put much thought and time in us. Our giftedness was not an afterthought. It was a part of God's plan to shape us for our role in the building of His Kingdom.

133. WHY DOES THE BIBLE RELATE SPIRITUAL GIFTS WITH MEMBERS OF THE HUMAN BODY?

Our human body represents *completeness*. It is made up of different parts. Similarly, the Body of Christ has different functions. We are gifted in different ways. Just as a physical body needs hands and feet and eyes and ears to enable it to function properly, so the Body of Christ needs those with different motivational gifts to enable it to function properly. We have *unity* through diversity.

> *For as in one physical body we have many parts (organs, members) and all of these parts do not have the same function or use, So we, numerous as we are, are one body in Christ, the Messiah, and individually we are parts one of another - mutually dependent on one another. (Rom. 12: 4-5 TAB)*

134. WHAT PART OF OUR BODY IS RELATED TO THE MINISTRY OF A PERCEIVER?

The Perceiver gift is the **eye** to the body, to clearly perceive the will of God. The Body counts on prophetic insight to accurately identify and proclaim the will of God. If it fails, how great is the darkness.

NOTE: We use the word "perceiver" instead of "prophet" because the word "prophet" is not one of the five Ministry Gifts here, but rather a vocal expression that can be anointed or quickened.

135. WHAT PART OF THE BODY RESPONDS TO THE SERVER?

The Servers are the **hands** of the body. They love to serve others; they are "doers." This is also referred to in I Cor. 12:28, as *the gift of helps*. These people love to be helpful, especially with hands-on involvement.

136. HOW DOES THE TEACHER RELATE TO A FUNCTION OF THE BODY?

The Teachers are the **mind** of the body. They love to research and communicate truth. They are gifted with intelligence and want to know the reason for everything. They check the foundation of truth to make sure it is solid ground.

137. HOW DOES THE EXHORTER RELATE TO A FUNCTION OF THE BODY?

The Exhorters are the **mouth** of the body. They love to encourage others to live a victorious life. Exhorters like to talk because they have a great faculty of speech to exhort, console or encourage.

138. HOW DOES THE GIVER RELATE TO A FUNCTION OF THE BODY?

The Givers are the **arms** of the body. They love to give time, talent, energy and means to benefit others. They are "contributors". Givers have great strength spiritually, a strong support to those who are in spiritual battle or out on the "front lines" sharing the Gospel.

139. HOW DOES THE ADMINISTRATOR RELATE TO A FUNCTION OF THE BODY?

The Administrators are the **shoulders** in the body of

Christ, carrying the load of leadership. They love to organize, lead or direct; they are facilitators, leaders. Wise administrators yoke up with Jesus so He shares the burden with them.

140. HOW DOES THE COMPASSIONATE PERSON RELATE TO THE HUMAN BODY?

The compassionate persons are the **heart** of the body. They are ruled by the heart, not by the head. They show compassion, love, kindness, care and mercy to others.

141. WHAT DOES IT TAKE TO BE A SUCCESSFUL MEMBER OF THE BODY OF CHRIST?

The motivational gifts can only be effective and successful if they are operated in **love**. The thirteenth chapter of Corinthians makes it very clear that without the motivation of **love** we have nothing.

> *Though I speak with the tongues of men and of angels, but not love, I have become sounding brass or a clanging cymbal. (I Cor. 13:1 NKJ)*

Being a successful member of the Body of Christ takes a wholehearted dedication and commitment to God as a **living sacrifice**. Our minds must be *cleansed and renewed daily* by prayerfully reading and studying the Bible and developing a personalized revelation of God.

I appeal to you therefore, brethren, and beg of you in view of (all) the mercies of God, to make a decisive dedication of your bodies - presenting all your members and faculties - as a living sacrifice, holy (devoted, consecrated) and well pleasing to God, which is your reasonable (rational, intelligent) service and spiritual worship.

Do not be conformed to this world - this age, fashioned after and adapted to its external, superficial customs. But be transformed (changed) by the (entire) renewal of your mind - by its new ideals and its new attitude - so that you may prove (for yourselves) what is the good and acceptable and perfect will of God, even the thing which is good and acceptable and perfect (in His sight for you).

For by the grace (unmerited favor of God) given to me I warn every one among you not to estimate and think of himself more highly than he ought - not to have an exaggerated opinion of his own importance; but to rate his ability with sober judgment, each according to the degree of faith apportioned by God to him.

For as in one physical body we have many parts (organs, members) and all of these parts do not have the same function or use.

So we, numerous as we are, are one body in Christ, the Messiah, and individually we are parts one of

another - mutually dependent on one another.
(Rom. 12:1-5 AMP)

142. WHAT MAKES MOTIVATIONAL GIFTS SPIRITUAL GIFTS?

Motivational gifts become spiritual gifts when they are activated by the Holy Spirit's power. It is wonderful to know that these *motivational gifts* or "in thee gifts" can be discovered through prayer, revelation or prophecy, but gifts remain natural, carnal, powerless unless they are *activated, brought to life by the breath of God.*

The Prophet Ezekiel was carried by the Spirit to a very large valley, filled with scattered, dry bones. The Lord asked Ezekiel, "Can these bones live?" Ezekiel answered, "Only you know that, Lord!"

And the Lord said, "Prophesy to these bones and say, 'O you old dry bones, hear the Word of the Lord!' "
(Ezek 37:3-4)

Ezekiel did as he was commanded and there was a shaking among the bones. He continued to prophesy until the bones had sinew and flesh. Ezekiel was then commanded to prophesy to the winds to blow upon the bones and when he did, breath came into them and they were alive. They stood upon their feet as a mighty army.

143. HOW DOES PROPHECY BY THE MINISTRY GIFTS IMPART AND ACTIVATE SPIRITUAL GIFTS?

Over the past 60 and more years, we have witnessed prophecy, prayer and revelation uncover the gifts God put into His people, but there has been very little life or activation of these gifts. What is the problem? We can discover our gifts and rejoice when we find them, but if they are not **activated** by the *breath* of God they will remain natural, carnal gifts - barren, lifeless; they cannot bear fruit.

The Church of Jesus Christ is being challenged, "Do you believe these bones can live?" Do you believe these bones can come together and be *unified*? Do you believe the army of the Lord will march together through the world with the power and demonstration of the Holy Ghost?

If you do, **Prophesy**! Prophesy to the winds that they blow upon the bones! Prophesy, prophesy!

144. WILL PROPHECY BRING LIFE TO THE BODY?

Yes! Nothing, absolutely nothing is made unless the Word of God makes it. Nothing is created, nothing is activated, nothing has life without the Word entering into it. Only the powerful Word of God can breathe life into dry bones. Is it any wonder we are encouraged, exhorted to "Covet to prophesy!"?

145. WHO CAN PROPHESY LIFE INTO DRY BONES?

This is the unique ministry of God's anointed Prophets who prepare the way of the Lord, to make ready a people for the Lord.

The scriptures promise the Lord will send the ministry of Elijah to earth before His return to energize His church and return the hearts of the fathers to the children, and the children to the fathers. That's restoration! That's revival!

And he shall go before him in the spirit and power of Elias, to turn the hearts of the fathers to the children, and the disobedient to the wisdom of the just; to make ready a people prepared for the Lord. (Luke 1:17)

*God has put hidden
springs within you,
that can satisfy
the deep longings
of your heart.*

CHAPTER TWELVE

The River Of God

*There is a river, the streams whereof shall
make glad the City of God, the holy place
of the tabernacle of the Most High.
(Psalm 46: 4)*

*D*uring World War II and the postwar years, many church leaders became very concerned about the spiritual drought many of their congregations were experiencing. The moving of the Holy Spirit had all but disappeared from many churches. It was so pronounced, ministers openly expressed alarm and concern. Our home church began a radio broadcast in the heat of World War II, to call, *America To Your Knees*. The program was successful: it addressed a current crisis. Thousands of mothers sent us the names of their sons in military service for prayer. We had an "Honor Roll" of hundreds of service men we prayed for daily.

Immediately after the daily radio broadcast, there was a fast-growing, well-attended prayer meeting. Prayers for peace, safety for the boys and a Holy Ghost revival went up to the Throne of God daily for seven years.

My mother was the founding pastor of our home church. She was a woman of prayer and great faith. The Lord spoke to her in a dream-vision of the night, in which she saw herself walking down a steep, rocky road, carefully carrying a little wooden bucket of sparkling, clear water. Off in the distance, there was a huge cloud of dust and the thundering sound of stampeding cattle and they were heading in her direction. As the cattle came closer, she saw their tongues were hanging from their mouths, swollen with thirst; they had caught the scent of the water in her bucket and they were thirsty and coming for a drink.

She quickly jumped off of the road and the herd of cattle passed by, but the danger was not past, for a second herd of cattle were bearing down on her from another direction. The thirsty cattle were determined to get their share of the sparkling, clear water that was in the bucket.

There was only one way of escape: slide down the steep slope of the ravine, and she did, just in time to keep from being killed. It was then she heard the sound of mighty, rushing waters. She turned and saw a vast river. There was water enough to satisfy all of the thirsty cattle who had followed her down the steep ravine.

She cautiously stepped around a huge bolder to find the source of this mighty, rushing river. There, at the mouth of the river was *Jehovah El Shaddai*, the breasted one. The crystal-clear water silently and freely flowed from Him, El

Shaddai, the nourisher who satisfies every thirsty, hungry soul.

She understood God's message: "Get ready, revival is on the way. The multitudes would be attracted to the silent river that she had found. She would lead them to El Shaddai, the Source of the water of life." And it came to pass.

THE SILENT RIVER

The Apostle Paul was the man God chose to reveal to the Church the secret of the *silent river.* God's *mystery* had been hidden *"even from the angels."* Men had sought to probe and decipher God's mystery for centuries, but God concealed it from "the rulers of this world," the spiritual powers which conspired to crucify Christ.

This mystery had been hidden for ages and generations. But now it was time: Jesus Christ had redeemed mankind by His death, burial and resurrection. God would reveal the mystery of the ages to His saints through the Apostle Paul. That mystery *is* Christ, but more, it is Christ indwelling His people. *"Christ in you, the hope of glory."*

Here is the revelation of the mystery: **We can be the temple, the dwelling place of Deity - Christ will live and dwell in us!**

> *For you are God's temple, the home of the living God, and God has said of you, I will live in them and walk among them, and I will be their God and they shall be my people. (2 Cor. 6:16 LB)*

146. WHY IS THIS REVELATION IMPORTANT TO US?

The Apostle Paul tells us in Colossians 1, the core of the Gospel is that **Christ**, "by whom and through whom all things were created, who is before all things and in all things, in whom God was pleased for all His fullness to dwell, the firstborn over all creation, the image of the invisible God - this Christ who has primacy over all things, in whom all things hold together, who is the head of the church - this Christ, who will stand at the end of time and be the final judge and triumphal Lord," *lives in us by the Holy Spirit*.

147. WHAT IS GLORY?

Glory is the Presence of God. Christ is the *brilliant radiance* of the divine glory. By means of Him the perfection of the nature of God is made known to men. ***This Christ, the Lord of creation, lives in His people.*** His dwelling in us is our *hope* of glory. His life and love desires to flow out from us *as a silent river* to a lost and dying world, to heal, to restore, to comfort, to save. That's glory!

148. MOSES ASKED TO SEE GOD'S GLORY. WHAT DID HE SEE?

Glory has two main lines of significance: *opinion* - what one thinks of himself, and *reputation*, what others think about him, which may shade into fame or honor or praise. Moses had a craving to see God, to come to grips with God as He was in Himself. In reply, God emphasized *His goodness*. The word *glory* might be rendered in this instance "moral beauty." God's glory is not confined to some outward sign which appeals to the senses, but that which expresses His inherent majesty, which may or may not have some visible token.

> *There's a River of Life, flowing out from me.*
> *It makes the lame to walk, and the blind to see.*
> *It opens prison doors, sets the captives free.*
> *There's a River of Life, flowing out from me.*
>   *(Unknown)*

149. HOW DO WE RESPOND TO CHRIST?

At our invitation, Christ enters our lives as an incorruptible seed that grows and matures until He becomes a part of our being by *indwelling us*. Through prayer we recognize and cultivate an awareness of His indwelling Presence and seek to give expression to His Presence in our life and work.

> *Being born again not of corruptible seed, but of incorruptible, by the Word of God, which liveth and abideth forever. (I Peter 1:23)*

150. DOES CHRIST'S PRESENCE BRING WHOLENESS?

Man's only hope or possibility for wholeness is to have Christ *dwell* in him. When Christ enters our lives and becomes a part of our being, we know wholeness of life with a *vibrancy* of spirit and joy.

> *Christ is the source of all wisdom and knowledge. We are complete in Him. (Col. 2: 3,10)*

151. WHAT IS OUR HOPE OF GLORY?

Glory is Christ entering our lives, becoming a part of our being, indwelling us, empowering and enabling us, so that we are not only the recipients, we are the *communicators* of the mystery. We are not reliant on our own energy, but that of Christ whose Presence works *mightily* within us.

> *Whom we preach, warning every man and teaching every man in all wisdom, that we may present every man perfect in Christ Jesus. (Col. 1:28 NKJ)*

152. HOW DO WE RESPOND TO HIM?

When we intentionally cultivate the awareness of the indwelling Christ, yield and respond to His Presence, He will grow and mature in us. We will know genuine *wholeness* and our ministry will be marked by an obvious spiritual quality that *genuinely* blesses others.

That Christ may dwell in your hearts by faith; that you, being rooted and grounded in love, may be able to comprehend with all saints what is the breadth and length, and depths, and height; and to know the love of Christ which passes knowledge, ***that you might be filled with all the fullness of God.*** *(Eph.3: 17-19 NKJ)*

153. HOW DO WE DISCOVER AND EXPLORE THE WELL WITHIN US?

Christ invites us to explore the well, the *silent river* within us. There are hidden springs, hidden streams deep in this well that will satisfy every longing of our heart. The *wisdom* and *knowledge* we need to develop our personality, our talents, our aptitudes, our "in thee gifts", are to be found in the well of God.

Now unto Him that is able to do exceeding abundantly above all that we ask or think, ***according to the power that worketh in us****. (Eph. 3:20)*

Spring up, O well, within my soul.
Spring up, O well, and overflow.
Spring up, O well, flow out of me.
Spring up, O well, set others free!

154. IS CHRIST COMING TO LIVE IN US A SPIRITUAL EXPERIENCE?

It was for me! One appointed Sunday morning in church, when I knelt at the altar to pray with members of the congregation, the Holy Spirit overshadowed me and I heard the Master's voice thundering through me with such intensity I felt my rib cage would explode with the pressure of His Words: *Thou too shall conceive and bear the Christ. All will say, What is this that has happened to thee?*

When I opened my mouth and repeated the words that were about to explode within me, the Words gushed out like a mighty torrent from the depths of my being. I had an overwhelming spiritual experience. The incorruptible seed of the Word of God was deposited in me. I met Him who is invisible and I was never the same again.

Prior to this time, I lacked the *desire* and *motivation* to serve Him. Family and friends marveled at the drastic change in me. Since that day, I have never doubted that Christ came to dwell and grow in me.

155. IS SUCH AN EXPERIENCE RECORDED IN THE SCRIPTURES?

Yes. When the Apostle Paul understood that God wanted to reveal His Son in him, he went to the desert to seek the face of God. He wanted Christ to be formed and matured in him, so that he might reveal Him to the world.

Paul encouraged the early Christians to let the indwelling Christ be formed in them.

*My little children, for whom I labor in birth **again**, until Christ be **formed** in you. (Gal. 4:19).*

156. IS THE FORMING OF CHRIST IN US A GRADUAL PROCESS?

I believe this is so. Spiritual growth is gradual. Christ indwells us by the power of the Holy Spirit, shaping our lives after His divine image, giving us the desire to partake of His divine nature.

Old things have passed away, behold, all things have become new. (2 Cor. 5:17 NKJ)

157. HOW WOULD YOU DESCRIBE THIS PROCESS OF MATURING?

This process of maturing is the exploring of the well of living water within us. Jesus referred to this when He spoke with the woman of Samaria. He said to her, *"If you knew the gift of God . . ."*

*But whosoever drinketh of the water that I shall give him shall never thirst: but the water that I shall give him **shall be in him a well of water***

157

springing up into everlasting life. (John 4:14)

158. WHY IS THE DEVELOPING OF CHRIST IN YOU A PROCESS?

We grow up in Christ. We discover Him and find ALL the treasures of wisdom and knowledge are in Him. We find *completeness* in Him.

> *For in Him dwelleth all the fullness of the Godhead bodily. And ye are complete in Him, which is the head of all principality and power. (Col 2:9-10)*

159. HAVE YOU EXPLORED THE SILENT RIVER, THE WELL WITHIN?

Yes! Hesitantly at first, because I neither knew *how* to explore it nor had any idea as to what I would find. Through prayer and worship, I *found* inner strength in the well of God, and springs in the valley. I also found resources of wisdom, knowledge and faith, but first I had to learn how to draw them from the well. I found *it is all according to the **power that worketh in me***.

> *Now unto him that is able to do exceedingly abundantly above all that we ask or think, according to the power that worketh in us. (Eph. 3:20)*

160. WHAT BLESSINGS DID YOU DRAW FROM YOUR "WELL"?

I found *love* to forgive, *peace* that passes understanding, *grace* to enable me to do what God called me to do and to be, *hope* when it looked hopeless, *guidance* when I lost my way, *patience* to wait for His timing, *understanding* of His will, *perseverance* to press forward, *strength* to endure, and *courage* to do what He asked me to do.

> *Flow out mighty river, flow out from my heart.*
> *Flow out mighty river, from me have your start.*
> *Flow out mighty river, to a dry, thirsty land.*
> *Flow out mighty river, at the Master's command.*
> *(Unknown)*

*Called people
have a strength
from within.*

CHAPTER THIRTEEN

Surviving Adversity

Endure your trials as the discipline of God,
who deals with you as sons. (Hebrews 13:7)

One of the great classic passages of the New Testament is found in the eleventh chapter of Hebrews. The dynamic and unforgettable definition of *faith* penetrates the heart when we read of the victory and spiritual success of those who conquered kingdoms, enforced justice, and stopped the mouths of lions by their unwavering faith.

However, one must be reminded that *persecution* is one of the outcomes of a life of faith. Not all the examples in this passage of scripture are of victory and success. There were others who endured mocking and scourging, chains and imprisonment. They were destitute, afflicted, tormented; they wandered over deserts and lived in caves and dens of earth. Yet, because of their faith, they shine as exemplars of endurance, perseverance, and courage.

How did they get such courage? *By faith*, **by faith**, *by* **FAITH!** This phrase echoes again and again, line after line in this chapter.

What was this faith? The Apostle Paul defined *faith* as: *The substance of things hoped for, the evidence of things unseen.* Faith is not an imaginary product of the mind or **rationalistic** dreams, but is firm, solid, of real existence. Faith is the solid certainty of that for which we hope, based upon reality and solid existence.

Where does faith originate? *Faith comes by hearing, and hearing by the Word of God.* Faith is based upon that which is tested and important. It is the power of God working through *all* the events of history to perform His mighty acts. This power may be unseen for awhile, but this faith turned loose in history by faithful prophets who spoke His Word, and believers who responded to it, has brought miracles upon nations and their history.

The Apostle Paul compares the Christian life to Christian athletes who are preparing to run a race. The stands are filled with the great athletes of the past, who have run their races and completed their events. They are now eager to encourage the new contestants. It is an active, watching throng shouting encouragement to those now struggling in their own events.

However, the Christian faith must have the necessary component of *discipline*. What was required of the faithful witnesses of the past will be required of this generation. There is a distinction between the *faithful called* and the *driven.* Christ separated people on the basis of their tendency to be *driven* or their willingness to be *called.* He dealt with their motives, the basis of their spiritual energy, and the sorts of gratification in which they were interested. He called those who were drawn to Him, and avoided those who were driven and only wanted to use Him.

This lesson, *Surviving Adversity*, is to help us face the difficulties in our life and evaluate them honestly: What motivates us? Where are we headed? Where are we going? What makes us function as we do? Are we *driven people*, propelled by the wind of our times, pressed to conform or compete? Or are we *called people*, the recipients of the gracious beckoning of Christ when He promises to make us into something?

161. WHAT IS REQUIRED TO WIN THE RACE OF LIFE?

In order to "win", every ounce of human and divine energy must be directed to the race. We must lay aside every distraction if we expect to survive adversity and achieve success. Anything less will cause us to fall behind the intentions and designs of our God. We are to *run with endurance the race that is set before us.*

162. WHAT CAN CAUSE US TO LOSE THE RACE?

Driven people are confident they have the qualities needed as they forge ahead. While basically they understand that unexpected, hostile events can occur and cause collapse, they are confident they can make it by sheer determination. They fail to realize many a great saint has been caught off-guard by a sloppy attitude toward relationships, disciplines of preparation, or commitment to excellence, only to find the situation lost and the opportunity gone.

163. WHERE DO WE GET THE STRENGTH TO WIN?

Called people have strength from *within*, perseverance and power that are impervious to the blows from without. Called people know exactly who they are; they have an unwavering sense of purpose and understand the need for unswerving commitment.

164. WHERE DO CALLED PEOPLE COME FROM?

Called men and women can come from the strangest places and carry the most unique qualifications. They may be the unnoticed, the unappreciated, the unsophisticated. Look at the men Christ picked: few if any of them would have been candidates for high positions in organized religion or big business. It is not that they were unusually awkward. It is just that they were among the ordinary. **But Christ called them, and that made all the difference.**

165. WHAT DOES IT MEAN TO BE CALLED?

It means we are drawn toward the beckoning hand of the calling Father and we live as a called person, rather than living according to drivenness.

166. CAN YOU GIVE US A SCRIPTURE EXAMPLE?

Yes. John the Baptist is a powerful example of a *called man*. Saul of Tarsus was a *driven man*. John's concept of life was by stewardship. He never owned anything. John thought like a steward: "How can I properly manage something for the owner until He returns?" He was not competitive, fearful or insecure. Saul reacted violently, lashing out against his perceived enemies when he became convinced that the preservation of his power and the survival of his position relied solely on himself.

167. CAN A DRIVEN PERSON BE CHANGED?

Most certainly. It begins when such a person faces up to the fact that he is operating according to drives and not to a call. That discovery is usually made in the blinding, searching light of an encounter with Christ. As the twelve disciples discovered, an audience with Jesus **over a period of time** exposes all the roots and expressions of drivenness.

To deal with drivenness, one must ruthlessly appraise one's own motives and values. It may require some humbling acts of surrender of things that are not necessarily bad, but have been important for all the wrong reasons. When he falls at the Master's feet to ask,

"What will you have me to do, Lord?" a *driven man* is converted to a *called one*.

168. HOW DOES A CALLED PERSON DEAL WITH ADVERSITY?

A called person understands, *Whom the Lord loves he chastens*. He draws closer to the Father to understand the discipline and make the necessary changes in his life. He is learning not to fear adversity but to think of it as an adventure in faith and to maintain an attitude of praise, knowing the adversity will work for his good.

All things do work together for our good *when we love and praise God and understand we are called and destined for winning*.

169. WHAT ABOUT SETTING GOALS?

Goals should be progressive and they have great drawing power. Every *called* person should set life goals to accomplish his mission in life successfully. Called people know who they are and where they are going. They are committed to the call of the Master.

Where there is no vision, the people perish: (Prov. 29:18)

170. HOW DO WE MAINTAIN A RIGHT ATTITUDE IN ADVERSITY?

The Scriptures teach *two-way prayer* with our heavenly Father. We seek Him in prayer and talk to Him about our problems. We wait to hear His wisdom, His counsel. When He speaks to us, His Word will create instant faith, for He speaks a promise of victory. Our faith in His Word will be tested, but in the timing of God it will produce the results we need to win.

171. WHAT IS MEANT BY THE BIRTH OF THE WORD?

In former MCS classes, we encouraged our students to seek a promise from the Lord that would calm their fears, and give them direction and faith to believe for certain victory. Fellow students prayed with those who were going through times of persecution, adversity or testing until they touched the Throne of God in prayer and praise.

The **rhema* word of God is born in our spirit while we are in His Presence. It creates faith in our spirit and releases the Power of God to fulfill it's purpose.

> *For the word of God is quick, and powerful, and sharper than any two-edged sword, piercing even to the dividing asunder of soul and spirit...*
> *(Heb. 4:12)*

So shall my word be that goeth forth out of my mouth: it shall not return unto me void, but it shall accomplish that which I please, and it shall prosper in the thing whereto I sent it. (Isa. 55:11)

*rhema: an alive, quickened Word from the Holy Spirit.
The Words that I speak to you are spirit, and they are life.
(John 6:63 NKJ)*

172. IS THE TIME OF ADVERSITY AN EXERCISE OF FAITH?

Most definitely. We learn of the Lord by the things we suffer. We learn experientially: He moves mountains. He stills the storm. Nothing is impossible with God.

The day will come when you will look back at this time of adversity and say, "Hallelujah, I'm a survivor! Praise God, I have survived adversity! Truly the Lord was with me through it all. I had fellowship with Him I would never had known but for the pressure and trials He brought me through".

*Many are the afflictions of the righteous, But the Lord delivers him out of them all.
(Psa. 34:19 NKJ)*

*Man's self-esteem
takes on new value
when he is reconciled
with God.*

CHAPTER FOURTEEN

The Sanctified Self-Image

*Don't copy the behavior and customs of this world, but be
a new and different person, with a fresh newness in all
you do and think... Be honest in your estimate of
yourselves, measuring your value by how much
faith God has given you. (Rom. 12:2,3 LB)*

*N*o society in history has motivated its people to be more concerned about *self-image* than contemporary American society. We have been led to believe that *if* our *self-image is positive*, the remaining areas of our lives will become well-adjusted and successful.

This rationale has resulted in the acceptance of the premise, "I'm OK, you're OK!."

However, the Bible also speaks about *self-image*. It declares the basic problem with *self-image* is **spiritual**. The solution to enjoying a positive *self-image* is ***living a life that***

173

is authentic. We must communicate **the real person and the actual lifestyle**. If the *self-image* is to be good, the life and the lifestyle must be good. Anything less than that would be *deceptive* and *hypocritical*.

THE CHRISTIAN LIFESTYLE

The Christian *lifestyle* has always been an issue of debate. The difference between a religion of *freedom* through the Spirit and a religion of *bondage* through the Law is still very relevant today. Since our religious experience and beliefs affect our self-image in positive or negative ways, we need to discover the *superiority* of spiritual religion over legalistic religion.

The Apostle Paul wrote that the words of the Old Covenant had become rigid laws, binding all those who sought life by attempting to keep them. He had no way of knowing there would come a day when sincere Christians would take the things he had written and create from them the very kind of *legalistic* Christianity which he opposed.

Paul always preached a *liberating* gospel. Those who were "in Christ" were free from the penalty and power of sin and ultimately free also from its very presence. In Christ they were made *free*; free to love everyone, free to celebrate their own unique gifts, and free to minister in unselfish ways to each other.

In this liberty there was joy, celebration and love that captured the attention of all. This joyful Christian lifestyle attracted even those who had lost their zest for life.

LEGALISM BREEDS SELF-CONDEMNATION

Paul warned the early church against *all* forms of legalism. Every effort to mix certain elements of the Old Covenant with the New Covenant is prostituting the gospel, undermining the work of the Spirit. Instead of freedom and liberty, legalism breeds *self-condemnation*.

The Old Covenant became the religion of struggling *to impress God with one's goodness*. Endless rules and regulations governed every conceivable area of life. Outward conformity and anxiety about appearance produced *spiritual pride and competitiveness*.

Legalists are always busy working out new sets of rules for new places, new circumstances, and new generations. Religion based upon a list of things Christians can or can't do will fade away into insignificant irrelevance. The *religion of the Spirit is permanent*.

NOTHING BUT THE BLOOD OF JESUS

The history of my home church includes a time when the members conformed to a rigid *Christian lifestyle*; we would never acknowledge or call it *legalism*. Because I was the pastor's daughter, I was encouraged to conform, to be an example to the flock, although my heart had never been changed. I had all the trappings of religion without ever knowing the love, joy, and freedom that is in Christ.

During my high-school years I was miserable. My self-image was that of a very *plain Jane*, who reluctantly carried a letter to school requesting to be excused from dancing and sport activities requiring athletic attire other than a modest-length skirt. I looked forward to graduating and becoming independent.

After graduation, I was hired for an office job and I was excited, that is, until I discovered two of my church friends were employed by the same company. I was trapped! I grudgingly settled down and resolved if I could not fight them, I needed to join them.

After I married and was the mother of four active little boys, I grew very weary, despondent and restless; something was *missing* in my life. I turned to prayer and Bible study, but I did not recognize *the* problem. I needed more than a *pious* life of church attendance and church laws. I needed to be *born-again*. I *needed* a personal relationship with Jesus Christ.

One day in prayer I heard the Lord pose a question to my spirit, "Do you believe the shedding of My blood *was enough payment* for the remission of your sins?" I was stunned! What a question! Of course I believe that!

"Then why do you keep turning and trusting in your *works of righteousness* for salvation, if you believe **My blood is enough?**"

I wanted to laugh. Surely, I could not have been hearing right. Does the Lord consider obeying our church laws, conforming to our rigid lifestyle and dress, *only works of right-eousness*?

The probing of the Holy Spirit would not go away. He repeated the question incessantly, "Is My blood enough? Is My blood enough? Is My blood enough?" I heard it day and night.

Finally, I broke and confessed with tears, **"I am wrong!"**

I had believed the obeying of our church laws would assure my salvation and bring me the favor and blessings of the Lord; but I was wrong! **Faith in the blood of Jesus Christ is all that is necessary for the forgiveness of my sins! Faith in the *works* of righteousness can never save us.** Suddenly, I knew the joy of sins forgiven!

I had never experienced the love, joy and peace in the Holy Ghost that now flooded me. What a difference! Rigid church laws and the trappings of religion had robbed me of the love, joy and freedom that is in Christ.

Now I knew I must live the new life I had found. *"Faith without works is dead". True repentance differs from remorse. Remorse* is sadness without action. Repentance is *action* in response to what the Holy Spirit is saying.

I went shopping to purchase whatever was necessary to change my *sad self-image* into *joyfulness*. On Sunday morning I dressed the children for church and my husband and boys sat in the car and waited for me. It was a most traumatic time. Modestly, but definitely, I dropped my *facade of self-righteousness* in obedience to the Holy Spirit's prompting.

The clock ticked away the minutes as I looked at my new image and cried, returning to my familiar lifestyle. An inner battle was being fought; I cried and changed my appearance back and forth until my eyes were swollen from tears.

My husband and sons patiently waited for me in the car; they understood the battle I was fighting. When I finally appeared they gave me a smile of approval and we drove to church.

How do I explain the reaction of the people who met me at the door? They were shocked! It was like *the shot heard 'round the world*. The telephone lines were hot all afternoon.

We returned to church Sunday evening and faced the same rigidity and pressure, until spontaneously, the song leader began singing an old hymn containing the words, "Grace - that is greater than all my sins." The Holy Spirit's Presence fell like rain. Hallelujah! A fountain of joy broke loose in me; praise to God exploded in my spirit. I knew I was free. Praise God, free at last!

The joy of the Lord was my strength and testimony. *"As the body without the spirit is dead, so faith without works is dead also." (Jas 2:26)* What an illustration! Everyone can easily understand the difference between a body which is dead, in contrast to a person who is alive.

I was a new creature in Christ Jesus. The evidence was the effervescent love, joy and peace of the Holy Ghost. The change in me stirred the congregation. There was a longing for *reality and peace*. The preaching was different, hard hearts melted in the Presence of Christ; the altar was filled with weeping men and women. Jesus Christ had come to meet His people and to set men free from the death and bondage of legalism.

A short time afterward the Charismatic Renewal spread across America. The Lord had faithfully delivered and prepared us to minister His *abundant life*. Our church attendance exploded with hungry people, eagerly looking for the *peace, joy, reality and balance* we now lived and shared.

173. WHAT IS THE SANCTIFIED SELF-IMAGE?

When we reflect the image of Christ, our *self-image* will be sanctified. The Christian whose life-light can dispel some of the darkness in this world has a sanctified, positive self-image.

When our miserable, self-condemning nature is expressed, we need to seek His help and forgiveness. When the Spirit of Christ comes into a person's life, he or she is able to understand God's message with his or her heart.

It is God to Whom we turn to judge our heart, to remove evil from us and to hold the reins that control our life. He alone has the answer to a good and positive *self-image*. When we reflect His image and likeness, our self-image will be perfect, sanctified and holy.

174. WHAT DID JESUS MEAN WHEN HE SAID, "DON'T JUDGE!"?

Every person has a blind-spot when it comes to recognizing his own shortcomings and faults. We can readily spot the faults of others, but we have real difficulty recognizing them in ourselves. Why? Because our heart is deceitful, always ready to put the blame for our actions on someone else.

Jesus knew all about sinful flesh. He became one of

us, yet without sin. "Don't judge another," He warned. "Wherein you judge another, you condemn yourself!" Why did He say that? We *expose* ourselves when we judge another. Why is it so hard for us to understand that we judge what we recognize as pride and shortfalls in others because they are also in ourselves? In other words: "It takes one to know one!"

175. WHAT COMPETES FOR POSSESSION OF MAN?

There are two master powers competing for the possession of man: **pride and humility**. Self-love, self-esteem and self-seeking are the essence of the life of *pride*. Pride shuts every man up to himself, bringing a death to all that is of God. Men are dead to God because they are living to *self*.

On the other hand, *humility* places man in an open heart posture before God. He thankfully receives the life-light and love of God. Every son of Adam is in the service of self until a humility from God enters his soul as the indwelling Christ.

176. HOW CAN WE IMPROVE OUR SELF-IMAGE?

The key to a good self-image is found in the image of what we are in Jesus Christ. In summary: we are a chosen generation, a royal priesthood, a holy nation and God's own special people, who were once not a people but are now the people of God. That description should enhance the self-image of *all* of God's people.

177. WHAT IS "THE CHOSEN GENERATION"?

God has extended His covenant blessings to all who follow Jesus as Lord. We are children of the King. That alone should improve our *self-image*.

178. WHAT IS A "ROYAL PRIESTHOOD"?

Through Jesus Christ we are called to be members of His Royal Priesthood. We have both the joy and responsibility to serve God and others. We have direct access to God. The Holy Spirit makes intercession for us and we can bring our offering of praise directly to God.

179. WHO ARE "CITIZENS OF A HOLY NATION"?

Believers are no longer strangers and foreigners, but fellow-citizens with the saints and members of the household of God.

180. WHO ARE "GOD'S SPECIAL PEOPLE"?

The Gentiles, who were once considered not a people of God, are now brought into Jesus Christ, to become citizens of God's new nation and to be *included* with those who are called *the people of God*. This has been the plan of God since the beginning of time: to have a people who are called by His Name.

> *But ye are a chosen generation, a royal priesthood, an holy nation, a peculiar people; that ye should shew forth the praises of him who hath called you out of darkness into his marvelous light:*
>
> *Which in times past were not a people, but are now the people of God: which had not obtained mercy, but now have obtained mercy. (I Peter 2:9, 10)*

181. WHAT RESPONSIBILITIES ARE INVOLVED?

Jesus taught that love for God is evidenced by love for our neighbor. Knowing God's forgiveness will lead us to share mercy. Experiencing God's love, we will, as a consequence, extend that love. We are called to proclaim or communicate the praises of God who has called us out of darkness into His marvelous light, to show mercy and love to our generation.

182. IS FAITH WITHOUT WORKS REALLY DEAD?

Yes. Our faith must include appropriate works. It is inconceivable for a person who is walking in the Spirit to say he has faith, if that faith is not translated into appropriate works of the Spirit by reaching out and responding to the needs of a brother or sister. Our faith must be accompanied by action.

> *If a brother or sister be naked and destitute of daily*

food, and one of you says to them, 'Depart in peace, be warmed and filled,' but you do not give them the things which are needed for the body, what does it profit? (Jas 2: 15-16 NKJ)

183. HOW DO WE LIVE BY FAITH?

We must move from deadness to *life*. We must follow Christ in *active* obedience. That is what it means to live by faith. Only when we have this "live" faith can we fulfill the Word of our Lord when He said, *Let your light so shine before men, that they may see your good works and glorify your Father in heaven.* *(Matt. 5:16 NKJ)*

184. DO ALL BELIEVERS HAVE A SANCTIFIED SELF-IMAGE?

No, but they *can* have a sanctified, positive self-image if their life-light shines brightly to dispel some of the darkness in this world. Wouldn't we be wise to look in the looking glass of God's Word and see whose image we reflect?

*God sees
the person
He will make!*

CHAPTER FIFTEEN

Beyond Ourselves

I can do all things through Christ, who strengthens me.
(Phil. 4:13 NKJ)

I t is not difficult for us to understand the fear and con-
sternation of the disciples of Christ when they were
told Jesus was going to leave them, He was going
away. Even though He assured them He would **not** leave
them alone and without help or comfort, but would send the
Holy Spirit to be with them, they were very uneasy and
deeply disturbed. They had lived and ministered with Jesus
Christ for more than three years. He was their teacher, their
spiritual strength and inspiration. Life could never be the
same without Him.

But Jesus knew they needed much more than just His natural presence and fellowship. If they were to continue His
ministry, and become His effective witnesses into all the

world, they needed *supernatural power from God.* They needed to be *indwelt* and *empowered* by the abiding presence of the Holy Spirit.

On the appointed day, the Feast of Pentecost, the wind and fire of God blew through the upper room where they were sitting and waiting, and the fire sat on their heads like burning tongues. Suddenly, the line of communication between God and man was opened wide and they began to prophecy in foreign languages the wonderful works of God. They were filled with the Holy Spirit, empowered and transformed to become *effective witnesses* for Christ.

This same *spiritual power* is available to believers today. By indwelling believers, the Holy Spirit *enables, equips and transforms* us into powerful and effective witnesses for Christ. It is God-given power and ability *beyond ourselves* to become and to do whatever we are called to do for Christ.

The Apostles and Disciples of Christ manifested this power in their ministry as they traveled across Asia. They preached the Gospel, and signs and wonders followed the ministry. *They turned the world upside down.* They boldly preached: **the Gospel of Jesus Christ is the *power* of God unto salvation.**

The Gospel power enables men and women to go and do whatever God requires of them, even *beyond their own natural ability and strength.* Whom God calls, He equips and empowers.

185. IS THE "MINISTRY" A DIVINE CALLING OR IS IT A PROFESSION BY CHOICE?

Any man or woman whom God has called to serve Him will be quick to tell you that no true servant of God chooses himself; it is the choosing of God. When Jesus Christ issues a call to serve Him, it is by personal invitation. When He conscripts, He enables. When He sends, He equips. That's why it would be very foolish to call ourselves into God's service, or to venture out into the spiritual battle *without* His clear commissioning.

> *Another thing to remember is that no one can be a high priest just because he wants to be. He has to be called by God for this work in the same way God chose Aaron. (Heb. 5: 4LB)*

186. IS THE PERSON GOD CHOOSES ESPECIALLY TALENTED AND ENDOWED?

There is nothing special whatsoever about men and women of God when they are called. All the external signs would seem to point in quite the opposite direction. Their faith is far from robust, their courage is minimal and their credentials in terms of family background and preparation are almost non-existent. But God sees the person He will make. God *knows* the power He will grant.

*For ye see your calling, brethren, how that not
many wise men after the flesh, not many mighty,
not many noble, are called: But God hath chosen
the foolish things of the world to confound the
wise; and God hath chosen the weak things of the
world to confound the things which are mighty;
And base things of the world, and things which
are despised, hath God chosen, yea, and things
which are not, to bring to nought things that are:
That no flesh should glory in his presence. (I Cor.
1: 26-29)*

187. ARE THERE BIBLE EXAMPLES OF GOD'S CALLING AND HIS ENABLING?

Yes. The Bible is filled with dramatic accounts of
God calling and equipping those He chooses. The
story of the call and equipping of Gideon is a prime
example of the ingenuity and sublime resourcefulness
of God. He loves to take the most unlikely clay to
mold his choice vessel. God delights to manifest his
sovereign power in the very midst of human weakness.

Read: Judges 6 and 7

188. IS HUMAN WEAKNESS A BARRIER?

Far from being a barrier to God, human weakness is the
first necessity for spiritual usefulness, provided only
that it leads to **obedience**, *in total dependence on Him.*

And he said unto me, My grace is sufficient for thee: for my strength is made perfect in weakness. Most gladly therefore will I rather glory in my infirmities, that the power of Christ may rest upon me. (2 Cor. 12: 9)

189. WHAT DOES GOD REQUIRE OF US?

Trust and *total* obedience! None of us can be useful to God in the public sphere if we are not putting him *first* in our private lives.

190. WHY DO WE FEAR TO OBEY?

We are still dominated by unbelief. We are very aware of our inadequacies and find it difficult to believe God could possibly use us. We can all spend plenty of time analyzing one another's weaknesses and inspecting our own deficiencies, but in the end that's a useless waste of energy. If God has called us, He is with us. If He is with us, what do we fear?

191. ARE OBEDIENCE AND TRUST ACTS OF FAITH?

Most certainly. It takes some tall believing to obey Christ's instructions. You have to *first* step into the water before you will see it part. You won't see the miracle of water becoming wine until you fill the water pots. You won't defeat Midian like Gideon did until you smash the idol Baal.

When God shows us a step we must take it, for the next door will not open until we have gone through the one already in front of us. And in order to do that, we have to *learn to trust* God with the consequences.

192. WHY ARE WE OFTEN DEFEATED BY FEAR AND UNBELIEF?

Could it be that many of us have *secret altars* hidden in our backyards that need to be pulled down before we can do anything for the Lord? We need to ask ourselves where we actually worship most? Is it at the altar of popularity or fashion; of money or status; of self-image or personal kudos?

193. WHAT IS THE REMEDY?

Total commitment is a **must**! *Tear down the altar... and cut down the wooden image.* This may well still be God's instructions to us, who need to cut through the pseudo- sophistication of much of our evangelical life, like a knife through butter.

When we look *beyond ourselves* and look to God, we see He is not looking for the most courageous man, the greatest warrior, or the most accomplished strategist. He is looking for a person who, knowing his/her own weakness, would *depend* all the more upon God for divine strength. Such a person is one whose faith could grow.

194. DOES GOD STILL USE ORDINARY PEOPLE?

Yes. God is always looking for men and women who are available to Him. Indeed, if we look at the record of God's mighty deeds in history, more often than not He has used very ordinary people through whom He has done so much, simply because they were so dependent upon Him.

195. DO WE HINDER THE WORK OF GOD BY OUR LACK OF TRUST?

Most definitely! Perhaps one of our dangers today is that we tend to look for men and women who have already been proved before we allow them any sort of responsibility. We have become so structured in our church organizations that, in many cases, we have stymied the initiative of the Holy Spirit. We discourage rather than encourage the young and inexperienced men/women and disqualify them for the roles that demand responsibility.

It is interesting to note: Charles Haddon Spurgeon, the great Baptist preacher of the nineteenth century, was pastoring a church at the age of seventeen. Pastor Lawson C. Hardwick, founding pastor of Christ Church in Nashville, Tennessee was only seventeen when he became a pastor.

196. WHERE CAN WE FIND POWER BEYOND OURSELVES?

The words of a prophecy delivered by Pastor Myrtle D. Beall in 1953, speak loud and clear of the equipping and empowering of God. May these inspired words bring you renewed faith:

The Lord has not given you the spirit of fear, but the spirit of love and power and a sound mind. You will be able to discern between the good and the bad, the precious and the vile and know that which is holy.

You will be led of the Lord thy God and he will make you as a nail in a sure place. You will have no uncertainty regarding the mind of the Lord, but you will have the spirit of the Rock within you, to enable you to stand in the storm and in the test.

The stream, the pure stream of God, shall flow through thee and from thee and all that has been mixture shall leave in the flow. You will not know yourself, but you shall know that it is not I, but the Christ that liveth in me. He doeth the work. It is he that doth flow forth into the wilderness and into the marshes and miry places, healing and leaving salt for preservation.

The stream is not of thee, my child, the stream is of the Christ within thee; He doeth the work. The fear of self, the fear of the weakness of your own nature shall leave in the stream of strength that flows from the indwelling One. Be not fearful but believing!

Pastor M.D. Beall - 1953

A vision or goal creates a reason to press forward.

CHAPTER SIXTEEN

Crossing The Finish Line

Wherefore the rather, brethren, give diligence to make your calling and election sure: for if ye do these things ye shall never fall. (2 Peter 1:10)

M y mission in writing this book is to evoke in you the knowledge that you are a special and unique person. Your life matters. It has purpose. It makes, indeed must make, a difference.

Every man and woman is born with a *particular gifting and mission for his or her life*. God has a purpose for you being alive and active on planet Earth. You must be free to express *who you are* from the depths of your being, to celebrate your created self in the service of God and humanity. I want you to say of your life, **"mission accomplished."**

If we fail to recognize or accept our special gifting, how can we *fulfill our God-given destiny*? Where do we go for help? Who has the answer to our quest for meaning and purpose for life?

As you have already read, I urge my readers first of all to be reconciled with your Creator! He *alone* knows the *purpose* for which He created you. He will help you as you *diligently* search to understand **who** you are, and **what** ma*nner of person you ought to be.*

Our own set of personality *weaknesses* and personal *problems* must be identified before they can be conquered. Victorious *overcomers* have experiences to share that help others recognize and develop their own potential.

Most people will agree *goal setting* is a must if you are to be successful and achieve anything worthwhile in life. It is proven that goals have drawing power; goals motivate us.

The Scripture speaks of **goals** as *vision. "Where there is no vision, the people perish" (Pr. 29:18).* A vision or goal creates a reason to press forward, to endure hardship, to keep a *positive attitude*, because it offers a reward or prize to be desired.

The Apostle Peter encouraged all **believers** to: *Give diligence to make **your calling and election sure**: for if ye do these things, ye shall never fall. (2 Peter 1:10)*

197. HOW DO WE MAKE OUR CALLING AND ELECTION SURE?

The Lord promises we will *know* what is His good and perfect and acceptable will for us *(our calling and election)*, when we present ourselves wholly to Him.

I beseech you therefore, brethren, by the mercies of God, that ye present your bodies a living sacrifice, holy, acceptable unto God, which is your reasonable service.

*And be not conformed to this world: but be ye transformed by the renewing of your mind, that **ye may prove what is that good, and acceptable, and perfect, will of God.** (Rom. 12: 1,2)*

198. WHAT IS MEANT BY "ELECTION"?

Election is the *destiny* that God, your Creator, has chosen as your life's *purpose*. Your *election* (destiny) never changes and is *revealed* to you by the Holy Spirit in many *different* ways.

199. WHAT DETERMINES OUR "ELECTION"?

We were *elected* by God before we were born, before we had a chance to do good or evil works. *Election* is not determined by our good or evil works, but by what God wanted and chose for us.

For whom he (God) did foreknow, he also did predestinate to be conformed to the image of His Son, that He might be the firstborn among many brethren. (Rom. 8:29)

For God had said to Moses, "If I want to be kind to someone, I will. And I will take pity on anyone I want to. And so God's blessings are not given just because someone decides to have them or works hard to get them. They are given because God takes pity on those he wants to. (Rom. 9:15-16 LB)

200. DOES THE BIBLE GIVE US EXAMPLES OF GOD'S ELECTION?

Yes, the Bible gives us *many examples* to help us understand God's *election*. Abraham, Joseph, David and the Apostle Paul are a few examples of men who were *elected* according to God's purpose.

*As concerning the gospel, they are enemies for your sake: but as touching the **election**, they are beloved for the fathers' sake. (Rom. 11:28)*

201. HOW WAS ABRAHAM ELECTED BY GOD?

The Lord of Glory appeared to Abraham when he was an idolater. Abraham was living in Mesopotamia when God asked him to follow Him.

... The God of glory appeared unto our father Abraham, when he was in Mesopotamia, before he dwelt in Charran. And said unto him, Get thee out of thy country, and from thy kindred, and come into the land which I shall shew thee. (Acts 7:2,3)

202. HOW DID JOSEPH LEARN OF HIS ELECTION?

Joseph was given *prophetic dreams* to reveal his future as a ruler.

> *And Joseph said unto (his brethren), Hear, I pray you this dream which I have dreamed: For behold, we were binding sheaves in the field, and lo, my sheaf arose, and also stood upright; and, behold, your sheaves stood round about, and made obeisance to my sheaf. (Gen. 37:6-7)*

203. HOW DID DAVID LEARN OF HIS ELECTION?

David was a young shepherd tending his father's sheep when he was summoned home and anointed by the prophet Samuel to become the King of Israel.

> *And Samuel said unto Jesse, Are here all thy children? And he said, There remaineth yet the youngest, and, behold he keepeth the sheep. And Samuel said unto Jesse, Send and fetch him: for we will not sit down till he come hither.*
>
> *And he sent, and brought him in. Now he was ruddy, and withal of a beautiful countenance, and goodly to look to. And the Lord said, Arise anoint him: for this is he. (1 Sam. 16:11-12)*

204. HOW DID PAUL LEARN OF HIS ELECTION?

Paul learned of his *election* when he was blinded by the Light, en route to Damascus to persecute Christians. Afterward, the prophet Ananias was sent to tell Paul that God had chosen him to be His witness of what he had seen and heard.

> *And I said, What shall I do, Lord? And the Lord said unto me, Arise, and go into Damascus; and there it shall be told thee of all things which are appointed for thee to do. (Acts 22:10)*

205. IS THERE A DIFFERENCE BETWEEN A CALLING AND AN ELECTION?

Yes. It is commonly understood that your *calling* is your destiny. For example, people say, "I am *called* to be a teacher, I am *called* to be a pastor" when, in fact, being the pastor or the teacher is an *election*, not a calling.

206. WHAT IS MEANT BY CALLING?

A *calling* is really a seasonal, temporary trial, testing or affliction to *prepare us* for God's *election* and conform us into the image of Jesus Christ.

"A *calling* signifies a *summons* by God to participate in a series of events and destinies whereby God executes His purposes." (Evangelical Dictionary of Theology).

*And we know that **all things** work together for good to them that love God, to them who are **called according to his purpose.** (Rom. 8:28)*

For our light affliction, which is but for a moment, worketh for us a far more exceeding and eternal weight of glory;

While we look not at the things which are seen, but at the things which are not seen: for the things which are seen are temporal; but the things which are not seen are eternal. (2 Cor. 4: 17-18)

207. HOW DID ABRAHAM'S CALLINGS PREPARE HIM FOR GOD'S ELECTION?

Abraham was told he would be the father of *many* nations, but he was not told **when** or **what** would take place before he would reach his destiny. As he received and obeyed *divine guidance*, he discovered his *purpose*, and *character* was built into his life. When he was 99 years old, he became the father of Isaac. The promise of being the father of many nations began to unfold.

208. HOW DID JOSEPH'S CALLINGS PREPARE HIM TO BECOME A RULER IN EGYPT?

Joseph was *called* to the pit, to slavery, to Potiphar's house, and then to the prison. Iron entered into his soul in the prison and formed his character. He had

occasion to use his gift to *interpret dreams* for the but-
ler and baker before he was summoned by the Pharaoh
of Egypt to interpret Pharoah's dream. Pharaoh set
him free and made Joseph the Prime Minister in
Egypt. Joseph's *election* was fulfilled.

> *Moreover he (God) called for a famine upon the
> land: he brake the whole staff of bread. He sent a
> man before them, even Joseph, who was sold for a
> servant: whose feet they hurt with fetters: he was
> laid in iron: Until the time that his word came: the
> word of the Lord tried him.*

> *The king sent and loosed him; even the ruler of the
> people, and let him go free. He made him lord of
> his house, and ruler of all his substance: To bind
> his princes at his pleasure; and teach his senators
> wisdom. (Psa. 105:16-22)*

209. HOW DID DAVID FULFILL HIS DESTINY?

David was anointed by the Prophet Samuel to be the
King of Israel when he was but a youth tending his
father's sheep. The Lord prepared him for his *destiny*
by serving King Saul as a harpist, to relieve Saul of the
evil spirit that tormented him. Praise and prophecy
flowed from David as he ministered comfort to King
Saul.

David's *callings* included the role of an armor bearer,
the slaying of the giant Goliath, and the threatening

wrath and vengeance of a jealous king. David spent seven years hiding in caves, rocks and the wilderness to escape King Saul's javelin and army. He even lived with Israel's enemies, the Philistines and the Amalekites, for a season before he was crowned the King of Israel. The songs and psalms David wrote in the darkness *of his callings* are a great source of comfort to us today.

But, that was not the end of David's *callings*. As David searched the Scriptures, he discovered his *destiny* was far greater than his present moment or *purpose in time*. David discovered his *election* and strength was *to build Zion*, the Tabernacle of David, to house the Ark of the Covenant.

> *To everything there is a season, and a time to every purpose under the heaven. (Eccl. 3:1 NKJ)*

210. CAN WE HOPE TO ENDURE THE CALLINGS THAT WILL BRING OUR ELECTION TO PASS?

Yes. The Lord will never give us more than He knows we can endure. As we survive each season of *calling*, we pass from glory to glory - to sow in one season and to reap *the benefits of our trial* in the next. You can't have a *testimony* without a *test*.

Don't take your eyes off of your goal *(election)*. Temptations will come to test you and entice you to abandon your *present calling*. Satan doesn't care if you stumble or sin, because he knows God will restore you. He wants you out of your *calling and ultimate election (destiny)*.

> *Many are the afflictions of the righteous, but the Lord delivers him out of them all.*
> *(Psa. 34:19 NKJ)*

> *For whom the Lord loveth he chasteneth, and scourgeth every son whom he receiveth.*

> *But if ye be without chastisement, whereof all are partakers, then are ye bastards and not sons.*
> *(Heb. 12:6,8)*

211. WHAT ABOUT OUR SPECIFIC GIFTEDNESS?

Be faithful and use the gifts the Lord has given you. Problems do not disqualify you from your election. Problems will bring experience and build character.

There are two classes of people on earth, the *fruitful* and the *unfruitful*. The fruitful are alive and reproducing. Don't become discouraged and stop practicing your gifts. You only have *what you use*. You may feel frail, fearful and imperfect, but somehow *in that earthen vessel is a treasure*.

Claim the day! You can be that *unique miracle* God had in mind at your *creation and redemption*.

For the gifts and callings of God are without repentance. (Rom. 11:29)

212. WHAT WILL KEEP US FAITHFUL TO ENDURE OUR CALLINGS AND REACH OUR ELECTION?

Keep your eyes on the prize! Target your weaknesses and fears; God will help you overcome them. When you are walking in the light of God's will, you are **walking in the Light**. Don't be afraid of change. Don't resist the unknown. Go forward and enjoy the freshness and creativity of God.

Creativity is the link for *entering* your life's mission (election). The absence of *creativity* will contribute to unhappiness and frustration, because you are blocked from self-expression. Learn to recognize, appreciate, and develop your *creativity*.

Creativity is: *"The process of becoming sensitive to problems, deficiencies, gaps in knowledge, missing elements, disharmonies... identifying the difficulty; searching for solutions."* - Paul Torrance

Rejoice! The Scripture says,

"The steps of a good man are ordered by the Lord: and he delighteth in his way. Though he fall, he shall not be utterly cast down: for the Lord upholdeth him with his hand." (Psa. 37:23-24)

213. IS IT POSSIBLE TO UNDERSTAND YOURSELF?

Yes. The Apostle Paul knew *who* and *what* he was; he understood himself. He suffered many severe trials as he passed through the *callings* Jesus Christ had ordered for his perfection and destiny. By God's grace, Paul *endured them all* and cried out victoriously, *"What will it be that will separate me from the love of God? Shall tribulation, distress, persecution, famine, peril or sword do it? No, I am more than a conqueror!"*
(Rom 8:35, 37)

It was obvious to Paul there was nothing in earth, heaven or hell that could **separate** him from his God-given *election* (destiny) and reward. Paul was more, *much more* than a conqueror. His last words were *triumphant* shouts of praise, as he crossed the *finish line*.

Hallelujah, I have fought a good fight,
I have finished my course,
I have kept the faith:
Henceforth there is laid up for me
a crown of righteousness,
which the Lord, the righteous judge,
shall give me at that day:
<u>and not to me only,</u>
<u>but unto all them also</u>
<u>that love his appearing.</u>
(2 Tim 4:7,8)

BIBLIOGRAPHY

Robert H. Schuller - "Believe in the God Who Believes in You."
Thomas Nelson, Inc. - Publishers 1989,
Bantam Books - July 1991

D. Stewart Briscoe - "The Communicators Commentary"
Volume I
"Genesis", Word Books, Publisher - Waco, TX - 1987

Naomi Stephan, Ph.D. "Finding Your Life Mission",
Stillpoint Publishing -1989

Lloyd J. Ogilive - "The Communicators Commentary Series"
Volume 5
Lloyd J. Ogilvie, "Acts" Word Book Publishers 1983

Lloyd J. Ogilive - "The Communicators Commentary Series"
Volume 11
Paul A. Cedar, "I and II Peter" Word Book Publishers 1984

Lloyd J. Ogilive - "The Communicators Commentry Series"
Volume I
Myron S. Augsburger, "Matthew" Word Book Publishers 1982

Don Baker - "The God of Second Chances - The Remaking of
Moses"
Victor Books, Scripture Press 1991

Dr. Bill Hamon - "Prophets and the Prophetic Movement"
Destiny Image Publishers 1990

Don & Katie Fortune - "Discover Your God Given Gifts"
A Chosen Book - Fleming H. Revell Company 1987

Note from the author:

Now that you have reached your goal of reading or studying through *"Understanding Yourself"*, you may want to read or study another book in the *Understanding Series*.

Understanding God & His Covenants

The ageless truths contained in this life-changing book continues to birth, train and establish disciples for Jesus Christ and promote church unity and growth. Experience the changing power of God thru the doctrines of Christ. Translations are available in Spanish, French and Russian.

Understanding the Master's Voice

Develop an intimate walk with Jesus Christ, by fine-tuning your spiritual ears. Understanding the Master's Voice stresses the importance of prayer, obedience, spiritual discernment and maturity to achieve a sound biblical foundation and spiritual balance.

These books are available at your local book store or Christian book store, or by writing the office of:

PeterPat Publishers, Inc.
P.O. Box 081816
Rochester, MI 48308-1816

For information concerning Rhema's teaching seminars, contact PeterPat Publishers, Inc.

Notes

Notes

Notes

Notes

Notes